Prai
IT'S NOT RO(

M000073291

"Susan Foster exemplifies the spirit of great leadership and has applied that same spirit to sharing her stories of what she's learned on the front lines of inspiring great teams. Through her example and teaching, you will move your own leadership to the next level."

Gail Larsen, founder, Real Speaking®, author *Transformational Speaking: If You Want to Change the World, Tell a Better Story*

"Good leaders train their subordinates and grow them into leaders. Great leaders mold those subordinates into competent, cohesive, high performing organizations. *It's Not Rocket Science: Leading, Inspiring, and Motivating Your Team* is a practical guide to help you build competent, cohesive, high performing teams."

GEN Eric K. Shinseki, U.S. Army, Retired

"This terrific book provides valuable insights and real tools leaders can use immediately to improve their organization."

James L (Jim) Jennings Former NASA Associate Administrator for Institutions and Management and Currently President, Omega Plus Inc.

"Not just another leadership book! This one will inspire empowerment and confidence in leaders at all levels of an organization with practical tips to help them improve their organizations. *It's Not Rocket Science* is a must read."

GEN (Ret) James D. Thurman, U. S. Army, Former Commander, United Nations Command, ROK US Combined Forces Command, U.S. Forces Korea

IT'S NOT ROCKET SCIENCE

LEADING
INSPIRING
AND MOTIVATING
YOUR TEAM
TO BE THEIR BEST

SUSAN C. FOSTER

WILSON
PRESS

WILSON
PRESS

Cover Design: John Matthews and Paul Thomas
Book Layout and Design: Paul Thomas/Light Now Media
Editing: Cynthia Kane & Kate Makled
Author's photo courtesy of Scott Steidley

Library of Congress Control Number: 2015949741

Print ISBN: 978-0-9964155-0-7
eBook ISBN: 978-1-942646-17-4

Printed in the United States of America

10 9 8 7 6 5 4 3 2 1

Dedication

To Don,
my love, soul-mate, and best friend.
As you said, it was easier to finish
than listen to you if I didn't.

CONTENTS

Acknowledgements

This book started out many years ago as a question: How can we learn to be great leaders so that people will follow us anywhere, just like the way I wanted to follow the best leaders I had? Every day, I see and read about and hear from leaders who want to do that, and I also see organizations and teams who struggle because they don't experience great leadership. I know we can change that.

In truth, so many people went into the making of the person who wrote this book, and I don't want to leave out anyone. I am so blessed. I lead a wonderful life because of all the lessons I've learned along the way, and it's solely due to a multitude of wonderful souls who taught me so much and supported me along the way.

To my husband and soul-mate, Don. Thank you for never doubting me. Not only have you always believed in me, but you've always supported me in anything I wanted to do. You teach me each day what it means to live fully. Your unwavering love makes life worth living.

To my wonderful family and extended family. Not one of you ever acted like you didn't believe I could do this. I love you.

To all my friends—past, present and future. If I start naming all of you who have meant so much to me, I will leave someone out. Please know you are my dear friends. I love you and appreciate you so very much, even when we don't see each other often.

To all the great Army leaders I worked for. I learned something from each one of you. You are deep in this book as you all taught me valuable lessons on leadership. Without them, I would not have been able to write this.

And to Martha Beck, who wrote *Finding Your Own North Star*, which started me on this journey. I only hope I help someone as much as your book helped me. Thank you from the bottom of my heart.

INTRODUCTION

Leadership is just getting people to follow you, and do it because they want to. For as long as I can remember, I wanted to be the leader. Over time, I often got the chance. Sometimes I was successful and people followed me, and sometimes I was a miserable failure. But I never lost my fascination for studying what makes people want to follow. Most of all, I studied leaders I had—the great ones, and the not so good. Every one of them taught me something.

I thought working harder and longer was the key to success, and that I could overcome what I viewed as others' perceived "weaknesses" if I just worked that much harder. After getting to the level where I had to get work done through others, however, working longer and harder just wasn't enough. I had to hone the skills I needed to get other people working for me to care about our success as much as I did.

I've struggled, as most of us have, with the frustrations of leading. Learning to master those so-called "soft skills" that are really so difficult. Sometimes I felt I just wasn't up to the task—not quite smart enough or powerful enough, or that it was outside my ability. But that's something difficult to talk about—no one wants to admit those things. And I also believed that one of the problems with leading others is that they usually couldn't perform tasks quite as well as I could. As a coach, I now know most of us have felt that way at one time or another.

I believe most of us who want to lead want to be great at it. We want to be successful and admired. We want to motivate our teams and organizations to do their best, and we want people to help us get promoted—or at least rewarded. Of course, promotions and rewards aren't the motivation for everyone. For some in professions of selfless service (such as the military, and some non-profits, etc.), it's all about our mission. We just want to know how to build a great organization and lead for the contribution we are making to the overall mission.

I've worked with and for some very smart people—yes, even actual rocket scientists—and I now know that being smart just isn't enough. The Oxford Dictionary defines rocket science as "an endeavor requiring great intelligence or technical ability; something difficult to understand." They deal with facts and data, and have computers to help them analyze complex ideas. They are very smart, but that doesn't mean they have an edge on you when it comes to being a leader. Leadership is all about people, and it's a job without formulas or predictable results—because everybody is different.

I believe that learning to be a great leader is not only possible, but it doesn't take great technical ability or advanced degrees. It's a skill that we can learn, practice, and get better at doing.

Through the years of leading, managing, and/or coaching literally hundreds of people, the vast majority who were smart—perhaps even brilliant—in their technical field, is that mastering those "people" skills is the most challenging thing a leader does.

Most of them really *are* brilliant. They are most often left-brained, tech-savvy strivers like I was. They believe in a data-driven formula for everything—and wish they had one to apply to their employees! They are frustrated that they are not able to quickly master getting their teams to follow them, and if they are business owners, they sometimes waste precious resources and time because they don't know how to get the most engagement from their employees.

When I have recommended great leadership books, many of my clients roll their eyes, especially after they have just finished telling me they are so busy and stressed that they hardly find time to be with their families, much less *read*. They tell me they just want some quick tips on how to lead better and get more motivation out of their people, and they invariably say, "What are some of the things you have learned?" And, "What are some of the things you have tried?"

I am quite sure the world doesn't need another leadership book. The last time I counted, there were over 130,000 on Amazon alone. I wrote this because I've seen these steps work time and time again. By giving you this book, I'm reminded of one of my favorite stories of all time, a story originally attributed to Loren Eisley, a noted American educator who taught at the University of Pennsylvania from the 1950's to the 1970's. I want you to be able to apply it to your organization, too.

It goes like this:

A man was walking along a deserted beach at sunset. As he walked he could see a boy in the distance, and as he drew nearer he noticed that the boy kept bending down, picking something up and throwing it into the water. Time and again he kept hurling things into the ocean. As the man approached even closer, he was able to see that the boy was picking up starfish that had been washed up on the beach and, one at a time, he was throwing them back into the water. When the man asked the boy what he was doing, the boy replied, "I am throwing these washed up starfish back into the ocean, or else they will die through lack of oxygen." "But," said the man, "You can't possibly save them all; there are thousands on this beach, and this must be happening on hundreds of beaches along the coast. You can't possibly make a difference."

*The boy looked down, frowning for a moment; then he bent down to pick up another starfish, smiling as he threw it back into the sea, and replied, **"I made a huge difference to that one!"***

I want you to claim your own leadership. I want you to feel you are making a difference. I want to give you some practical tools I've learned, most often the hard way, and help equip you in getting the best from your organization or business. When I say "best" I'm talking about motivated employees, strong and highly-functional teams, smoother-running organizations, and fewer "people" problems.

I'll give you real-life examples, including my own, of struggles, successes, and failures (mine as well as others'), and some worksheets you can use to help you build your leadership "muscles" so that they become natural to use. I want you to not only benefit from my lessons and failures, but I want you to feel you can do this "leadership thing" with more confidence and less stress.

4

I want you to feel that you can be the kind of leader who:

- Has a reputation for getting results by building high-performing teams that anticipate and plans for change, and are highly functional among themselves.

- Gives and gets no "surprises"—the expectations are clear.

- Is prepared when issues arise so they can be taken care of in a timely way.

- Is recognized by peers and managers for getting great results.

- Is respected by peers, managers and employees for being the kind of leader they want to be.

We are going to talk about what works, what doesn't, and how to get it all done in a day's work—and still have time to catch your kid's ballgame or meet your friends for dinner.

CHAPTER 1
The Problem

A successful man is one who can lay a firm foundation with the bricks others have thrown at him. – **David Brinkley**

The number one question I'm asked by the leaders I coach is some variation on, "How do I motivate people to have the same work ethic I do?" Sometimes they cannot describe what they want more from their employees, but they know they want them to be more like them.

Sometimes we don't realize that what we are doing might be demotivating.

Rosslyn was the Team Leader in charge of a large and complex task of transferring several thousand employee payroll records, to set up a central payroll center in another state. With payroll scheduled every two weeks, transferring it—and getting everyone paid on time during the transfer—meant every detail had to be well organized, with contingency plans for anything that could go wrong. After all, she knew the worst thing you can do is fail to deliver a paycheck! She had planned meticulously for months, and was proud to present her plan to the Assistant Vice President (AVP). The meeting was going splendidly. Rosslyn had it laid out in meticulous charts, and had rehearsed every question that the AVP might ask. When the briefing was finished, instead of the accolades she expected, the AVP's only comment was, "This all looks good, but I want you to know I'm watching you. Your career is on the line here if anything goes wrong."

Rosslyn was my employee, and this was one of those times where I look back and know I should have said something. I actually couldn't believe I had heard it right. What a great example of how **not** to motivate an employee! When this happened, I saw my star employee begin "second guessing" herself at every point of the conversion. Although it all turned out just fine, she was never quite as excited or motivated again.

And I wondered, "When was the last time I had been guilty of not motivating my team?"

I have always been interested in what makes people "tick." What makes some employees so great and others, with the same opportunities, not so great? And how could I get them all to be, or strive to be, one of the "great" ones?

As one of those leaders who was either working 24/7, or thinking about work, I was always rather startled that everyone didn't want to work as hard as I did. That's the problem, right? Getting people to do what we want them to do, and getting them to *want* to do it like we would. I used to believe that if everyone would just work as hard as me, our organizations would run like clocks—or computers. There wouldn't be the problem of our people sitting around "chit-chatting." More work would just get done. My boss would think I was a great leader, and I'd be steadily promoted, or at least commended for leading well.

So how do we get the most out of people who don't seem as interested in accomplishing great things at work? What about team members who don't even see what those things are? How do we take a group of people, make them work together as a team, and accomplish more together than any of us could do by ourselves?

Some say it's getting the right group together. I had one leader who just moved people around when someone complained about them and their abilities. His attitude was, "Don't waste your valuable time on them." Invariably, however, all the "weaker" (read that less-experienced, trained and/or less motivated) employees would end up in one division or team. And usually that team would also be rotated every year or two, so one manager didn't have to keep them forever. On the other hand, what made them weaker and less motivated? Was it lack of training? Weakness of character? The fact that they had never been given standards they understood? Or perhaps because of being on a team where they were "out of sight—out of mind?" Although Rosslyn was a star employee, all my employees haven't been. But they all had something to contribute.

I've had leaders who I'd follow anywhere, and I've had leaders that I'd never work for again. But the great leaders: what was it about them that made me want to work all night, if that's what it took, to put out a product they would notice and appreciate? And how can we instill that in the people who work for us?

Our People: We Can't Do Without Them

Our organizations and business run with people. Their time, energy, ideas, creativity, etc., are at the core of every organization and business. Few businesses run without them, and even sole proprietorships that have only one employee must have customers, who are also people. They are both a cost and an asset.

If we could be superhuman and do everything ourselves, that would make it all easier, wouldn't it? But since people determine how well a business is run and how much money is made, learning to lead them—and lead them well—just makes good business sense.

Picture your organization as being a huge machine with hundreds—perhaps even thousands—of gears. Some are big wheels (no pun intended!), some are smaller wheels, and some are tiny nuts and bolts. Every one of them is important for the machine to run. Think of the leader as the finest of oil spread throughout all those gears and wheels to make it run smoothly.

You know what? Our big machine is not doing so well.

This powerful resource (our people) is less productive and unhappier in their work today than ever.

We spend money to hire them and train them, they are at the hub of our business—and yet they are unhappier and less engaged than ever before. Employee engagement is defined as "the extent to which employees commit to something or someone in their organization, how hard they work, and how long they stay as a result of that commitment."[1] In other words, it's how hard they work, how great their ideas are, and whether or not they leave after we've paid to train them.

The latest Gallup report from their ongoing study, "The State of the American Workplace: Employee Engagement Insights for U. S. Business Leaders," which provides insights into what leaders can do to improve engagement and performance, claims that *only 30 percent* of all employees are actively engaged—contributing creatively to their work teams. Twenty percent more are actively disengaged (spreading discontent and toxicity to everyone else). *And fully 50 percent* are just not engaged—getting paid, but not inspired, not creating— just "there."[1]

Not only are the resources of this creative talent drawing salaries, but according to the study, those employees not engaged have higher health care costs and cause a higher number of quality defects.

Half of the lifeblood of your organization—are not happy, not inspired, and not contributing.

They are leaving their jobs—or trying to—in record numbers.

And Gallup attributes this to the quality of their bosses.

Why It Matters

I assume we would all prefer our people be happier. But more than happy, what if this translated into more money and higher profits? Research suggests that it does.

Dr. Noelle C. Nelson, a clinical psychologist and author of the book, *Make More Money by Making Your Employees Happy*, explains that a study from the Jackson Organization, says "companies that effectively appreciate employee value enjoy a return on equity & assets more than triple that experienced by firms that don't." She also said that when looking at Fortune's '100 Best Companies to Work For,' their stock prices rose an average of 14% per year from 1998-2005, compared to 6% for the overall market." [2]

It stands to reason that if people are our biggest resource—as well as cost—then employees who aren't engaged are costing money, and that's important.

But it's also costing us our health.

I believe our jobs are one of the biggest stressors we have in our life.

A National Institute of Occupational Safety and Health survey reported 25% of respondents viewed their job as their number one stressor, and said it affected their health complaints more than family or financial problems.

The Attitudes in the American Workplace VII study reported that 80% of workers are stressed, and 14% had felt like striking a co-worker.

Every client I have has cited stress on the job as their big issue, and a large majority attributes it to the leader.

But What About Me?

So you might be thinking by now, "So what about me? I'm sorry they are unhappy, but I'm way too busy and stressed—and picking up their slack—to be able to deal with that." Ask any leader nowadays and they will say they have more than they can possibly accomplish. Too many projects. Too much stress. Too few employees. Too little time.

Gotcha. Busy leaders are busier than ever.

The Center for Creative Leadership (www.ccl.org) reported in one white paper, "The Stress of Leadership," that 88% of leaders reported that "work is a primary source of stress in their lives and that having a leadership role increases the level of stress."[3] They also reported that lack of resources and time are the most stressful leadership demands—the pressure to do more with less.

You may be tired of trying to juggle your job and your personal life, trying to retain your best talent, and figure out how to handle the ones that aren't so talented. On top of that, your business is changing, and sometimes you can't even grasp what that change is, but you see it in the guidance (or lack thereof) from your boss. You may not feel you have time to fix your "people problems," much less time to develop them. But you want to. You want to be known as a transformational leader, one that gets the best out of their employees. One who is the leader everyone wants to work for. We'll get you there. Stay tuned.

So, what do we know?

We know people are unhappy.

We know our organizations are suffering as a result.

We know that most employees think they do a good job, and will say it's the leader's fault if things fail.

We know employees don't feel engaged, interested, creative, and appreciated.

We know we as leaders feel too busy, too stressed, and too overwhelmed to fix that.

So if the data tells us that leadership matters to the bottom line, and our goal is to be a great and transformational leader and improve the lives of our team, how can we become the successful leaders that make the difference and turn around this trend?

How can we be the leaders that everyone wants to work for? That's the discussion of these next few chapters, with just a few steps that will make the biggest difference.

The 99%

I was always amazed that others didn't necessarily seem to realize how much harder I was working than they were. Like some other leaders, I sometimes concentrated on the few who didn't do everything like I thought it should be done. One thing I discovered as I progressed from one leadership level to the next, and observed leaders who I worked for: Ninety-nine percent of the people who worked for me didn't get up in the morning and say, "Let me see how I can mess up Susan's day today." Even when comparing employees who were less trained and experienced with those who were better trained and more experienced (and having counseled numerous employees), I have met very few who didn't think they were doing a good job.

Sometimes I didn't think they were doing such a good job, but they believed they were. What's up with that? And what was the answer? Berating them? Giving them a poor performance review? Withholding awards? By the way, I never saw any of these methods be effective.

More than just doing a job, however, what we really want is

commitment, not compliance. We want them to be as committed as we are. We want our team members to *want* to be creative, to *want* to come up with great ideas, and to *want* to think strategically. This wanting translates to seeing things that are going wrong before we have to tell them, and taking the initiative to fix problems proactively.

Does leading them differently really matter? Let me tell you where it did.

Suzanne's new job was a good opportunity for her to show what she could do. She had been named Director for a division that was failing—it had gone through three other Directors in as many years, and its primary project had never gotten off the ground. Having been warned that the people were "weak," she proceeded without further investigation to do all the planning for the now-late project. She drafted all the plans, timelines, and even wrote the contracts to ensure they were done right. Working literally night and day, she didn't even enjoy her week-long vacation in Florida. A multitude of details swirled in her head the entire week, and her husband remarked that she had not seemed to enjoy just being with him. How could she? There was so much to remember, and a major project milestone was coming up when she returned. When she did return, to her dismay, she realized *not one* of her people understood her intent or her detailed plans. Since she couldn't continue without them, she spent valuable time coordinating plans, teaching them what she had done, and what to do to launch the project.

Contrast Suzanne with Tom. He wasn't sure how he even landed this job as the new Division Chief, as he heard there were 118 people vying for the same position. The previous

Division Chief had retired due to health reasons. Although Tom didn't know the Vice President who was his new boss, he knew he reported directly to the CEO. He heard he was tough, but he was sure he could please him. After the first day, Tom realized he knew little about this Division's mission, but obviously the people on his team did. They had been running it pretty successfully, even with their boss being out so much. The first couple of weeks were a whirlwind—getting updates from his new staff on their duties and learning the way his boss wanted things to go. Customers were scattered in several states, so his employees traveled a lot, and there was little time to manage them face-to-face. Delegation had always been difficult for Tom, but he soon realized he wouldn't be able to keep up with every detail like he always had. Within a few weeks, he worked out a system where he could get the highlights of what they were doing and any issues they had into key summary points. Sure enough, the day came after about six weeks where the CEO called and asked for an update on a project. Tom's boss was on travel and the responsibility fell to Tom. He passed that meeting with flying colors.

These stories of "before and after" are true. Although most names in this book have been changed to protect privacy, Suzanne and Tom are actually the same person—me.

In the "before" I wasn't so successful leading the team. In the "after," I was able to shine.

Let's talk about what made the difference, what I learned, and how it can help you get what you want from others. Not in a manipulating way, but in a way that's free from strategies, games and stress.

We'll talk about five simple steps (I didn't say always easy) that will make all the difference. You can always do more, but if you can use these steps consistently, you will transform your team in a way you never dreamed possible. I've seen it happen time and time again:

Step 1. Make a Personal Connection

Step 2. Build the Trust

Step 3. Say What You Mean and Mean What You Say

Step 4. Did You Hear Me?

Step 5. Praise and Feedback

And if you make it through all of that—there's a little something extra to help you shine.

CHAPTER 2
Step 1: Make a Personal Connection

"The day soldiers stop bringing you their problems is the day you have stopped leading them. They have either lost confidence that you can help them or concluded that you do not care. Either case is a failure of leadership." – **Colin Powell**

People don't care about you or what you want until they know you care about them. How do you let them know you care about them? By establishing a personal connection with them, finding out what motivates them, and what they want.

What Is A Personal Connection?

Making a personal connection simply means getting to know the people on your team in a way that shows genuine interest, beyond just business. Today, most of our work is intellectual and services; it is built people-to-people. Although most of us think that strength and tenacity is what makes us attractive as leaders, research indicates that when evaluating people on whether or not to trust them, we pick up on warmth over strength.[4] Making a personal connection with the people on your team means finding out what they want, what they need, what their values are, and who they are as real people, not just in the workplace.

John was the CEO of a major technology company. He started it with a friend from college. He had hired most of the staff, and as the company grew, he had hired the head of each of the six divisions. John and his senior executives had worked out business issues at retreats and in the office, but they had also become good friends. Their kids played ball together, and they spent many great evenings at family picnics, cookouts and school events. After a few years, the company grew into a major competitor in their area. There came the time when the Board of Directors voted to make a major change into a new market that would affect every sector in the company. It also became apparent that four of the division heads did not have the skills to move them in this new direction.

John said that the only reason the company was able to weather this difficult time, losing four senior people, and integrating new ones, was the friendships and personal connections he had built with these four people. Because of the relationships they had built over the years, these leaders were able to transition into other companies and ease new leaders in without tearing the company apart.

Why We Don't Connect

Connecting with the people who work for you at a meaningful and person-to-person level is one of the most difficult things my clients tell me they do; however, it's the first step because it's the foundation to transforming any team.

Why is it so difficult? First of all, when we have stressful workdays, it's easy to fall into the belief that people are just supposed to do their jobs and not whine about them, and that establishing a relationship with them has no place, especially if you are brought up in a company culture that fosters that. Most of my leadership-developing years were spent working for the U. S. Army, and I certainly believed that people should do their jobs and not complain. But this was also an advantage for me. Although the culture taught me not to make excuses, it also showed me a culture whose leaders—the great ones who really make a difference—make it a point to learn who their soldiers are as people. It just makes sense for them—after all, knowing everything they can about that soldier helps them know how to lead them better, and can make a life-and-death difference in a combat situation. Most of us aren't in that kind of stress every day, so we lose sight of how much it matters.

Secondly, it's difficult because we feel that although it might be nice, it just takes too much time. A few leaders have even suggested it might be too "touchy feely" and perhaps even weak, something hard-charging executives certainly can't be seen as.

It turns out it's none of that—it's a well-accepted leadership trait that companies are looking for.

Emotional Quotient (EQ), Not Intelligence Quotient (IQ)

Companies have discovered something that has changed the face of executive leadership training in the past 20 years, and is even changing the way they hire executives. In 1990, John D. Mayer from the University of New Hampshire, and Peter Salovey from Yale University wrote a paper that was made popular in the *New York Times* on a new concept called "emotional intelligence." They defined the distinction from the intelligence we know in IQ tests ("the intellectual capacity of the individual to act purposefully, think rationally, and effectively deal with their environment") from emotional intelligence, which they defined as the "ability to monitor one's own and others' feelings and emotions, to discriminate among them and to use this information to guide one's thinking and actions."[5]

The author of the article for the *Times*, Daniel Goleman, PhD, went on to write a book on the concept in 1995 (called *Emotional Intelligence and Social Intelligence: The New Science of Human Relationships*) which began an entirely new, and still expanding, area of leadership concepts and research in organizations. We now have many business cases for the concept, and it has become well accepted that leaders need emotional intelligence as much as they need problem-solving skills. Many companies now use emotional intelligence/emotional quotient assessments in hiring, training and evaluating leaders.

To ensure it's not just a fad and that solid business data is captured, the Graduate School of Applied and Professional Psychology at Rutgers University now has a Consortium for Research on Emotional Intelligence in Organizations (CREIO) that researches business cases, and some companies use emotional quotient (EQ) evaluations in hiring for leaders. Here are just a few of the cases they cite.[6] You can find many others and more information at their website listed in the Resources Section of this book:

- The United States Air Force used EQ tests to select recruiters (the Air Force's front-line Human Resources personnel) and found that the most successful recruiters scored significantly higher in the emotional intelligence competencies of Assertiveness, Empathy, Happiness, and Emotional Self Awareness. The Air Force also found that by using emotional intelligence to select recruiters, they increased their ability to predict successful recruiters by nearly three-fold. The immediate gain was a savings of $3 million annually. These gains resulted in the Government Accounting Office submitting a report to Congress, which led to a request that the Secretary of Defense order all branches of the armed forces to adopt this procedure in recruitment and selection.

- Experienced partners in a multinational consulting firm were assessed on the Emotional Intelligence competencies plus three others. Partners who scored above the median on 9 or more of the 20 competencies delivered $1.2 million more profit from their accounts than did other partners, a 139 percent incremental gain (Boyatzis, 1999).

- An analysis of more than 300 top-level executives from 15 global companies showed that six emotional competencies distinguished the stars from the average: Influence, Team Leadership, Organizational Awareness, Self-confidence, Achievement Drive, and Leadership (Spencer, L. M., Jr., 1997).

- At L'Oreal, sales agents that were selected on the basis of certain emotional competencies significantly outsold salespeople selected using the company's old selection procedure. On an annual basis, salespeople selected on the basis of emotional competence sold $91,370 more than other salespeople did, for a net revenue increase of

$2,558,360. Salespeople selected on the basis of emotional competence also had 63% less turnover during the first year than those selected in the typical way (Spencer & Spencer, 1993; Spencer, McClelland, & Kelner, 1997).

- In a national insurance company, insurance sales agents who were weak in emotional competencies such as self-confidence, initiative, and empathy sold policies with an average premium of $54,000. Those who were very strong in at least five of eight key emotional competencies sold policies worth $114,000 (Hay/McBer Research and Innovation Group, 1997).

- Research by the Center for Creative Leadership has found that the primary causes of derailment in executives involve deficits in emotional competence. The three primary ones are difficulty in handling change, not being able to work well in a team, and poor interpersonal relations.

An entire industry has grown up around evaluating and using your EQ. You and your team can take an assessment to help you understand how much emotional intelligence you use (EQ evaluation instrument information is included in the Resources Section).

Emotional intelligence focuses on four basic competencies— self-awareness, social awareness, self-management, and social skills—that influence the way we handle ourselves and our relationship with others. Salovey and Mayer argue that these human competencies play a bigger role than cognitive ones in determining success in life and our workplace. Before EQ became a popular term, we knew them as "people skills."

All of these competencies are important in learning to be

great leaders, and they are just behaviors. We can choose to develop them and use them, or we can choose to ignore them at work or in life—at our peril, in my opinion. Imagine if John's company executives had not built these personal connections so many years before serious challenges came along. What turned out to be a success story could have been much different.

Why We Overlook Personal Connections

Let's face it: personal connections bring up something that's sometimes difficult to talk about in the workplace: emotions— and something else called *empathy*.

Empathy is the feeling that you understand and share another person's experiences and emotions—the ability to share someone else's feelings. Sometimes we get it confused with sympathy, which is feeling sorry or pity for someone but not necessarily understanding the problem or predicament they are presently in. Empathy is trying to understand how you would feel in their shoes. In their bestselling book, *Getting to Yes*, Roger Fisher and William Ury say, "It is not enough to study them like beetles under a microscope, you need to know what it feels like to be a beetle."

And this is the crux of why making a personal connection with your team might be overlooked as a sound first step: because empathy and emotions are two things that hard-charging leaders are uncomfortable with. Some of them are uncomfortable because they see it as too "touchy-feely," and one client even sheepishly referred to it with me as "girly." Another expressed to me that when it was time to "kick butt," it was hard to do it if he had a personal relationship with his employees.

We can make a personal connection and still be strong and competent. We can still maintain high standards. When we get to the chapter on trust, you will see that when you have that connection *and* when people trust you, you can have those difficult conversations when people aren't meeting standards and still maintain that relationship—like John did.

Denying that we have emotions that are with every one of us all the time, even (and especially) at work, is to deny an important part of ourselves. The fact is, emotions are neither good or bad—*they just are*. They are with us every day. We can't take them off like a coat.

Where do they come from? Our deeply-held values (more about that in Chapter 7).

"We are creatures of strong emotions who often have radically different perceptions and have difficulty communicating clearly," says Fisher and Ury.

Emotions can cause us to feel angry, fearful, offended, and can make us operate toward others with a "blind spot" (an aspect of our personality that is hidden from our own view). Or, used to our advantage, they can help us let our team know we care about them as people. Acknowledging and understanding our own emotions helps us choose which ones to use, as well as how and when.

Just like John, making that personal connection well before any issues come up is the foundation of a relationship that will get you through the challenges you are sure to encounter.

Richard Scherberger, owner of Executive Leadership Skills, International, and one of the best organizational consultants I know, says it like this: "We will always have emotions, attitudes and feelings all the time. The question is: which ones are we going to select? EQ says: We are most powerful when our emotions and thoughts work together. I say: we are most powerful when we understand our thoughts can be managed to influence our feelings and emotions!"

Make Some Deposits

In his famous book, *7 Habits of Highly Effective People*, Stephen Covey told a story about the importance of making emotional deposits in relationships. He explains that, like a bank account, healthy relationships thrive when there are more "deposits" made than there are "withdrawals." In other words, you have more positive encounters with someone than you have negative ones. Examples of deposits could be something as simple as spending a few minutes in the morning, asking how your employee is doing, how he or she enjoyed the weekend, or how the son or daughter is doing in Little League. It can include a regularly-scheduled meeting where you just listen, or it could be an impromptu stop-by on the way to lunch. Whatever it is, it is the foundation for a relationship with that person. A relationship can help weather your work life's withdrawals with a healthy account.

Covey goes on to say that if very few deposits are made in the relationship, but withdrawals are constant (negative feedback, criticism, etc.), it can damage the relationship, and can often leave it unrepairable. When challenges arise—and they most assuredly will—your relationship is "overdrawn." It's hard to get commitment (or cash!) from an overdrawn account. The relationship becomes one-sided, with one doing all the giving.

Waiting until it's time to give negative feedback before you make that deposit doesn't work either. That's called manipulation, and not only is it transparent to the employee, as it would be to you if it were your boss, it can further damage the situation.

Is it hard to make the time? Sometimes it is, but it's well worth the effort.

My client, Sylvia, and I spent about 50 minutes during a recent session talking about all the things she was concerned about—strategy, and meeting the goals and objectives for her team. Toward the end of the call, when we started discussing her people challenges, she said, "You don't understand. I am just too busy. I just don't have time to connect with my people."

"Sylvia," I said, "We have talked for over 50 minutes on all the things you can do to be a better leader—setting goals, meeting your project milestones, the technical work. Did you realize that most of these things can be delegated? The one thing that can't, however, and the thing that is the most important in helping you become a great leader is connecting with your people personally, on a regular basis. You just can't delegate that."

She said she never considered that. When she made that effort and tried it out, she told me it made an immediate difference in her team.

Great leaders make time for it. Richard Branson, founder of The Virgin Group, and author of the book, *The Virgin Way: Everything I Know About Leadership*, makes time for it, and says that "visiting your staff in their natural habitat as often as is practicably possible is huge for you and for them. I often find this to be one of the biggest gaps in the make-up of otherwise accomplished leaders."

If the owner of 400 companies makes the time for it, I guess we could give it a try! He goes on to say about his managers who don't:

"They are all busy-busy people, with big important things to do, big important people to meet and big decisions to make and big....well you get the picture. To close this priority circuit, making the commitment every week to spend some quality time with your most important assets—your people— is every bit as critical as any other entry in your diary. A tall order perhaps, but it is a discipline that, if you can pull it off, brings huge paybacks on multiple levels, often in the most remote places where you probably never imagined you had levels of influence."

How We Can Do Better

"OK," you say, "I'm buying it. So how can I make personal connections with my people?"

Here are some ways you can work that personal connection in to your work life that I invite you to try. You will come up with others. When you do, I'd love for you to send them to me at susan@susancfoster.com so I can share them (and give you credit, if you like) with other leaders.

- Schedule a regular time to meet one-on-one. This is not performance evaluation time—it's time to just chat and get to know them. This is sometimes uncomfortable for introverts, but just begin by saying you appreciate all they have been doing and ask what's going on in their lives. You won't have to do much talking yourself. You may want to jot down one or two facts about them, such as hobbies, number of children, or their volunteer work, and keep that for future meetings. I know one leader who carves out a couple of hours a few times a month, and has her admin schedule each direct report for 15-30 minutes each where they can discuss anything they want.

- Schedule a "brown bag" luncheon—in your office if you have the space, or in a conference room if you don't. I did it one division at a time, and it helped tremendously in getting to know people on a personal level. I told them they could ask me anything, and I would tell them if I could. But I really just wanted to get to know them. I opened with this: "What is the one thing you would do if you couldn't work here and you could have any job you wanted?" I was amazed at how much people opened up, and you will find out things you never would have otherwise.

- Send them a personal card on their birthday. The leaders I remember as being the best did this, even though they were very busy people. One time my executive assistant got card stock that was blank inside, and I just wrote a short note wishing them a happy birthday. Or you can have a printed card, and add a short note like, "Glad you are here. Thanks for all you do."

- Schedule an hour to walk around and visit employees in their workplaces a couple of times a week. Just a knock at the door and a minute or two of, "How are you today?" counts.

Did you notice a theme here? You have to schedule it. I found that scheduling the time for making a personal connection was the only way it got done. The days will invariably get taken up with meetings, to-do lists, and unforeseen calls. I invite you to start by carving a couple of hours a couple of times a week until it gets routine; then you can evaluate the amount of time you need.

I have clients who are very introverted who find it difficult to sit one-on-one with employees. I remind them that an introvert just means you get your energy in other ways, and dealing with people may mean you then take a walk by yourself, or close your office door and regain that energy—but it will pay off over and again in ways you hadn't realized.

There is an old story that goes like this:

A Hindu saint, who was visiting river Ganges to take a bath, found a group of family members on the banks, shouting in anger at each other. He turned to his disciples, smiled and asked:

"Why do people shout in anger at each other?"

The disciples thought for a while, one of them said, "Because we lose our calm, we shout."

"But, why should you shout when the other person is just next to you? You can as well tell him what you have to say in a soft manner," asked the saint.

The disciples gave some other answers but none that was satisfactory. Finally, the saint explained...

"When two people are angry at each other, their hearts distance a lot. To cover that distance they must shout to be able to hear each other. The angrier they are, the stronger they will have to shout to hear each other to cover that great distance.

What happens when two people fall in love? They don't shout at each other but talk softly, because their hearts are very close. The distance between them is either nonexistent or very small."

The saint continued, "When they love each other even more, what happens? They do not speak, only whisper and they get even closer to each other in their love. Finally, they even need not whisper, they only look at each other and that's all. That is how close two people are when they love each other."

He looked at his disciples and said. "So when you argue do not let your hearts get distant. Do not say words that distance each other more, or else there will come a day when the distance is so great that you will not find the path to return." —Unknown

Making a personal connection with the members of your team is the foundation for everything you want from them. Why do we want someone to connect with us in a personal way? Because it makes us feel like we matter. And when we feel we matter, we will follow that leader through thick and thin.

Personal connections matter even more than communication, because communication is a *skill*, and connection is a *feeling*. And remember, how you make people feel goes a lot further in getting the best from them than strictly focusing on what's in their job description.

How Am I Doing On Making Personal Connections?

1. What do I know about each one of my team members/employees that is personal?

2. How often do I connect with my employees on a personal level?

3. How often do I connect with my employees in their work environment?

4. What is my plan on increasing my personal connection with them?

How Well Do I Know My Employees?

1. Do they have children? What are their ages?

2. What are their hobbies? What do they like to do when they are not working?

3. Are they into sports? What are their favorite teams?

4. What's a favorite meal? Do they like to cook?

5. What's one great experience they have had they would like to repeat?

6. What's a goal they would like to accomplish within the next three years?

A downloadable copy of this worksheet is available at www. susancfoster.com/book so that you can keep one for each employee on your key team.

CHAPTER 3
Step 2: Building Trust

Trust is the glue of life. It's the most essential ingredient in effective communication. It's the foundational principle that holds all relationships.. – **Stephen Covey**

When you ask someone what the most important thing is about a leader they will often say, "Someone you can trust." We may not always know how to define trust, but we always know it when we see or feel it.

What Is Trust?

Trust is the firm belief in someone or some thing's integrity, ability or character. When we trust someone, we have confidence in them. We can rely on them. We know they "have our back." What about a lack of trust? We are suspicious—of their motives and agenda—whether they are being nice towards us or not. We don't have a confident feeling about them, and we don't want to work for them.

As the leader, you can be a great strategist, have a compelling vision, be a great communicator, be a technical whiz, and get lots of press, but if people don't trust you, you will never be a leader who makes a difference. On the other hand, if your people trust you, they have better morale, loyalty, and pro-ductivity, and the organization has less turnover.

We could make a case that this is even more important to a foundation of a leader than making a connection, because it's impossible to make a genuine connection when people don't trust you.

Warren Buffet said, "Trust is like the air we breathe. When it's present, nobody really notices. But when it's absent, every-body notices."

Let's talk about what it is, what it isn't, and how we can do it better.

Why A Lack of Trust?

Failing to trust others is rampant in today's society and our businesses, from financial institutions, to religious institu-tions, to our government. But it doesn't have to be that way— and it doesn't have to be in your organization. When trust is broken, it takes a long time to recover.

The executive team seemed to be finally coming together. Spirits were improving. We had weathered a major disaster that had brought world attention. We were at the end of a se-ries of studies and inspections, and had undergone grueling self-assessments of our leadership issues. It was pointed out over and over again in these assessments that our culture did not foster listening to bad news. We had a couple of meetings where things had gone well.

One particular morning, one of our leaders told everyone he

wanted us to close the doors and have honest and frank discussions about what was going on, so we would never again lull ourselves into a false sense of things going right when they really were not. When it came time to hear from each person, they did begin to open up; however, when the meeting began to go on a little longer than usual, he started to get a little impatient. When the next person brought up an issue, the leader cut him off sharply, saying we needed to just move on, embarrassing the executive in front of everyone.

A few weeks later, the executive team had an off-site planning meeting. A prominent author on leadership was our keynote speaker and guest. The leader of our organization started off telling everyone this was our most important planning meeting of the year. He encouraged everyone to be forthright and open up about our issues. The meeting was an all-day event that was probably most impressive with the lack of participation among every member of that team. A fellow team member and I discussed it on the way back that day: the trust had been broken that morning in the conference room. There was no one on that team who believed our leader, and I heard several people express that the comment on "open and forthright" was for the famous guest.

In Stephen M. R. Covey's great book, *The Speed of Trust: The One Thing That Changes Everything*, he says that trust is the most powerful form of motivation and inspiration in organizations, and that it's the ultimate source of influence. On the other hand, he also talks about low trust slowing down communication and decision making, and hindering relationships and results. Covey believes that mistrust is more the norm than the exception. He cites research that found in organizations: only 51% of employees have trust and confidence in their senior management; only 36% believe leaders are honest and act with integrity; over a 12-month period, 76% of employees had observed illegal or unethical conduct on the job! [7]

David Horsager, who is the author of *The Trust Edge: How Top Leaders Gain Faster Results, Deeper Relationships, and a Stronger Bottom Line*, says that trust affects a leader's impact and a company's bottom line more than anything else. "One of the biggest mistakes a leader can make is to assume that others trust him simply by virtue of his title. Trust is not a benefit that comes packaged with the nameplate on your door. It must be earned, and it takes time," he said in an interview with Forbes.[8]

It doesn't matter how impressive your credentials or how high up in the company a leader is, trust is all about relationships—and relationships are best built by establishing genuine connections. It's the foundation of building a great team or organization. We want commitment, not just compliance, right? If your team trusts you, they will work long hours, brainstorm creative ideas to solve problems, and go the extra mile to make you look good. Without trust, you get teams that go through the motions, but lose heart.

Brian Tracy said, "The glue that holds all relationships together—including the relationship between the leader and the led—is trust, and trust is based on integrity."

How We Can Build Trust?

We build trust the same way we lose it—by our behavior. It

can be earned with something as simple as a five-minute conversation at the coffee pot with an employee who has been staying late to work on a project. This conveys that you care not only about the project, but also how that employee is doing and acknowledging their hard work.

I like to think of being trustworthy as being credible, reliable, and fair. Let's talk about how we can do those things and what I mean by them.

Credible—Bad News Doesn't Get Better With Age

Edward R. Murrow said, "To be persuasive, we must be believable; to be believable we must be credible; to be credible we must be truthful."

Credible

- Tell the truth

- Be willing to hear the truth from employees

- Honor your commitments

- Admit your mistakes; don't cover them up

Tom was in a meeting with a few key executives. They were preparing for a conference call with a U. S. Congressman on an issue in the budget the Congressman was concerned about. This was a government agency, and the Congressman's office had been given a story on the background by the agency. A newspaper reporter had called the Congressman's office, however, to verify a different set of numbers and story received from other sources. Before the conference call, Tom's leader announced what the "story" would be, so "everyone will be on the same page." Then she discussed the answers to some possible questions from the Congressman. This caught Tom by surprise. This wasn't just a positive spin—the story they were giving the Congressman that morning was untrue.

The room got quiet; it was obvious everyone was uncomfortable. Tom summoned up the courage to say, "Let's go ahead and tell the truth and take our licks on this. Too many people could be asked that could refute this story. Don't you think we'll look better just to say we made a mistake?" The decision went with the leader, and the phone meeting went as planned. Just as Tom had predicted, a few weeks later the story his office told was indeed found to be untrue, and the agency garnered the Congressman's ire for a long time to come. The trust was broken.

We all make mistakes. Just as in the story above (which is true), those mistakes most often come back to bite us, especially in this day of media stories and computers to check facts.

Sometimes truth telling is hard. Leaders often don't get rewarded for it. But being willing to tell the truth as you know it, and allowing your employees to tell you the truth without reprisal, is just basic to gaining their trust. When it's not true, someone always knows it.

When I say "truth" here, I am talking facts. I realize that someone else's "truth" might feel different than mine. When we deal with ourselves, our customers, and our employees authentically, however, we know when we have spoken the truth as we know it to be.

Allowing our employees to be able to tell us the truth, even when it's uncomfortable, is just as important. We may not want to hear it because we are too busy to deal with it—but if they are to trust us, they have to be able to know we will hear them.

As for keeping commitments: if you say you will do it, then do it. It's as simple as that. I had an employee who was a great analyst, but famous for telling everyone what they wanted to hear. She often ended up having to go back and recant what she had promised, which undermined trust for the entire organization.

As one of my old bosses used to say, "Bad news doesn't get better with age!"

Reliable—None of Us Know it All

- Share information

- Give credit to your employees when things go right, and take the blame when they don't

- Maintain confidences

Sharing as much information as you can just makes good business sense. We have all heard "knowledge is power," and our employees want us to have power in an organization—to feel they are part of that power because they are "in the know." You build credibility and reliability through the shared power of keeping them in the loop.

Conversely, I have known leaders who believed knowledge was power, and if they knew and you didn't, they were more powerful. I hope I can impress upon you that this just isn't the case. I had a boss who used to withhold just one piece of information when we were working on a project, and see if we "discovered" it during our analysis. It didn't take us long to realize he couldn't be relied upon to give us all the information we needed. This did not engender trust, as you can imagine.

Giving information and showing your employees you can be relied upon to share what you know—as much as you know— won't erode your power, but enhance it. The people who work for you just cannot do as good a job for you if they don't know what you know. Of course, there are times when you can't tell them. In those instances, I always said, "I'll always tell you what I can tell you, and I'll tell you if I can't tell you." That way, they knew when I said, "I can't tell you right now," that it meant I couldn't violate a confidence.

Another downside of not sharing information is that employees often believe silence in an organization means things are bad, and they had better be dusting off that resume and looking around. I was often surprised at what the "rumor mill" brought to my door because of what people assumed without good information, and it was usually information I should have provided. Take every opportunity to tell them as much as you know about where the company is going, where it's growing, what the industry trends are, and your goals for them.

Giving out information openly and candidly, when you can, is the best way to get employees and colleagues to keep you advised about what's going on, too.

Just as sharing information is what great leaders do, taking the blame when there's a problem, and giving out the praise when there is some being spread around, is another way we enhance our power and consolidate our trust with them. And please, never, ever blame an employee in public for a mistake. Always deal with that in private. When your employees know you will take the blame in public, and talk to them in private when it's really their fault, they will not only trust you—they will follow you anywhere.

You know how you feel when you tell something in confidence and that person betrays you? Your employees need to know that you will not reveal confidences, no matter what.

Fair—What's Good for One is Good for All

- Make decisions based on facts and merit, not rumors and "favorites"

- Involve others when analyzing an issue

- Be consistent—employees can depend on you being the same today as yesterday

- Refuse to condone illegal and unethical behavior

- Ensure all employees are meeting standards

Patty worked for a manager who was unhappy with her work. Patty often made mistakes that others had to clean up, and the manager came to talk to me about moving her to another office. She had counseled her several times, and Patty promised to do better. As we discussed what could be done, her manager and I talked about all the employees and what accounts they were responsible for. We discovered that Patty's accounts were more complex than most of the other analysts, and that the person who had trained her had been out sick a good portion of the previous few months. We both realized that Patty just didn't have the adequate training to handle what she had been given—and it was *our* fault. We moved her to a simpler account, and sent her for additional training. As a result, within six months, Patty received an award from her customer for her outstanding work. After that, she volunteered for an off-site assignment where her work just shined. I learned a valuable lesson about judging an employee fairly without all the facts.

I know all stories like this don't have a happy ending; however, it often does when we look into facts about a situation. It's human to assume we know someone's talents and failings, as well as their motivations. When our employees know we will look at all the facts in an unbiased way, they begin to trust us—even if it doesn't always go their way. And when we don't, we will develop a team that may not tell us everything we need to know.

When employees know we base decisions on facts and data, and use empathy and fairness, they will also trust us to do our best in a challenging situation where no decision is really favorable.

Looking the other way when some employees consistently come in late, or take a late lunch, is a good way to erode trust in the others. You don't have to be a hard-nose, but if it's all right for some of them, you should go ahead and tell everyone it's all right for them, too.

I have had leaders tell me they couldn't have conversations on standards with employees. My response is that establishing trust with them is the *only* way you can have those caring, frank and meaningful conversations—both when things are going well, and when they aren't. In the example with Patty, *fair* meant giving her work according to her abilities and developing her abilities to take on more difficult work.

While we're on the subject of meeting standards, part of making connections and building trust is being able to have conversations when challenges come up—often difficult for leaders because they aren't always pleasant. Having those regularly-scheduled meetings we talked about makes that easier, because you can calibrate on what they are doing and how.

"Always tell the truth, as accurately as you can and within the context of the situation," says Judith E. Glaser CEO of Benchmark Communications, Inc., Chairman of The Creating WE Institute, Organizational Anthropologist, and consultant to Fortune 500 Companies. She says that we often skirt the truth because we feel fear—fear that the truth will lead to broken relationships and feelings of rejection.

When our employees trust us, we have already established a relationship that lets them know our intentions. Only then can we have those truthful and direct conversations where there is shared commitment to improvement without hurting the relationship we have established.

One great idea from a former boss of mine: He had meetings at the end of each project, small or large. It's called "3 Ups and 3 Downs." Ask each person to give you 3 Ups —things that went well, and 3 Downs—those things that, if we had had perfect knowledge, we would have done differently. Most times, the employee will tell you everything they did that was wrong, and how they would do it differently next time to ensure things would go smoother. Every time I have tried this, I never had to point out what went wrong. This also establishes trust, in that they can talk about new steps to improve the goals and process, and get feedback from you.

One other thing: while we want to gain trust with our employees, we must also learn to trust. This can be difficult, especially when our company culture may not foster trust, and we don't see our leaders role-modeling it for us. We also don't trust out of fear—fear of telling the truth to our boss, fear of reprisal, fear of not being given the right opportunities, fear that people aren't telling the truth.

Trust with your team is something you can establish, but what about those times when trust is broken and you need to repair it? You may have even inherited a team where the previous leader wasn't trusted, and no one will trust you until they see how you handle situations first.

"You can fix [broken trust], but it doesn't happen quickly," says Dennis Reina, a corporate consultant who, along with his wife, Michelle Reina, wrote the book, *Rebuilding Trust in the Workplace: Seven Steps to Renew Confidence, Commitment, and Energy.*"

"A breakdown in trust or communication doesn't mean we are weak leaders or dysfunctional employees," says Michelle Reina, who is also a corporate consultant. "It just means we are human beings. We have a choice with how we respond, and many times I'll see a leader who hears there was a trust issue, and they will just want to move past it and forget about it.... But if you don't take a look at it, this will cause bigger problems in the future."[8]

Even if you don't see it modeled in your organization, I encourage you to build trust in your team. It's the only way to

CHAPTER 3

get any trust back. As a leader, you can have no greater re-source than a high-performing team of people who trust you. They will produce their best work and you will transform your team. Without it, it just won't happen.

How Am I Doing On Building Trust?

1. Do my employees and co-workers trust me? How do I know?

2. Does every employee, from my newest or least-paid, feel a part of the team and know his/her ideas are encouraged?

3. Do I seek ideas and opinions different from my own?

4. Do I act and speak consistently? Do my employees and co-workers always know what to expect from me?

5. Do I always tell the truth as I know it, in a way as to improve the situation?

6. Do I expect and accept nothing less than complete integrity from my subordinates, especially my managers?

7. Do I confront difficult issues rather than letting them continue?

8. Do I do what I commit to?

9. Do I keep confidences?

10. Do I admit my mistakes? Do I take the blame for things that don't go well and deal with them?

11. Do I treat everyone fairly and apply equal standards and privileges to everyone?

CHAPTER 4
Step 3: Say What You Mean and Mean What You Say

"The problem with communication is the illusion that it has occurred. **–George Bernard Shaw**

I n my opinion, the subject of communication has been done a *lot*. There are colleges that offer majors in it, companies built around it, and thousands of books on it. On the other hand, all those resources exist because communication is something we do every day and it's something we often don't do well. In fact, communication skills is probably the number one goal most of my clients say they want to work on.

What It Is, And What It Isn't

Good communication means the message you send is received by those it was intended for, in entirety, the way you meant it. It's as simple as that. When this happens, people are more likely to respond in a positive manner. What I mean by that is when you say something with a certain intent, such as you want an extra piece of pie, that's what you get. And good communication is more than words—it's also tone and body language.

This chapter is going to talk about a very small part of the subject—ways you can ensure you communicate so that you get the results you want from your team. This is a skill you can work on the rest of your career and life—and probably will—but I want you to benefit from some early successes and feel confident that you can do it well. We will also talk about giving employees a reason to be here (vision) and setting clear expectations so that we get exactly what we want, without misunderstandings, and a team who is behind you 100 percent without you having to be a micromanager. Then we'll talk about the communication tool we love to hate—the staff meeting!

Why It's Important

If you speak and write so that what you say is meaningful, understandable, and has impact, there is little you can't accomplish. Most of the misunderstandings and failures I've had as a leader happened because I didn't clearly communicate my wants, needs, and intentions. I didn't give the context, the intent, or my expectations. And I dare say most of the arguments we have in our personal lives are because we didn't do those things. Many of our arguments and disagreements occur simply because one of us did not communicate clearly.

We want our teams to understand what we want so valuable resources (their time, our time, and money) aren't lost to going down the wrong track. In many cases, miscommunication is just a time waster. It can be, however, more serious, such as making a project impossible to complete on time and within budget, or failing to meet customer or stakeholder expectations. Taken to the extreme, in industries such as aviation, for example, communication errors can even cost lives.

Do you remember the Air Florida Flight 90 that took off from Washington National Airport (now Reagan) going to Fort Lauderdale in January of 1982? Conditions were snowy in the District of Columbia that day. The aircraft had not been de-iced properly, and it didn't have its engine anti-icing system properly activated. This caused the instruments to freeze and fail to register the correct readings. So, while the cabin crew thought that they had throttled up sufficiently for takeoff, in actual fact they didn't have enough power. As they set off down the runway, the first officer noticed that something was wrong with the plane's instruments and that it wasn't capable of getting airborne. His attempts to communicate this were brushed off by the captain, who ordered the takeoff to continue. The plane crashed into the 14th Street Bridge, killing 78 people, including four motorists. Later, reports showed that there was sufficient space for the aircraft's takeoff to have been aborted—if only the flight crew had been communicating better.

So Why Don't We Do It Well?

We know it's important—we do it all day, every day. Yet we still don't always do it well at work. There are lots of reasons, and these are only a handful:

- Ego, pride and generational gaps: We see things from our own personal "filters" and values. This can happen in ordinary situations, but when people become angry with each other, the likelihood of a barrier is greatly increased—almost to the point that it is inevitable.

- Organizational hierarchy: We may believe that since the other person works for us, their opinion must not be as valuable as ours.

- Differences in experience and perspective: When we say something, we know what we mean, but with other people's experiences and background, they don't hear the same thing. This is especially true when we work with people from other cultural and language backgrounds. When we work with people from different cultural backgrounds, economic positions, and religious beliefs, an understanding (not necessarily an agreement with) their views are important.

- We are uncomfortable with the subject, especially around performance.

- All parties don't have the same information. Gathering information needed to deal with conflicts can be time-consuming and expensive. In some cases, time isn't available to get all the facts. Because we may have information the other party doesn't, we are assuming they can understand what we mean when they don't.

- We put off conversations. Because we don't always feel we have the skills to handle delicate or difficult conversations with employees, we tend to put off these conversations, which is often unfair to the other employees.

- We are rushed. We get busy and don't take the time to plan the communication. We don't give the context of what we want—the what, when, where and why.

The better we realize and understand our own barriers, the

better we will be at saying what we mean—and meaning what we say.

How We Can Do Better

Communicate A Shared Vision

People are drawn to working for leaders who speak about the future in such a way that moves us. I know I am. I used to think that having and communicating a clear vision for where our organization was headed was a nice-to-have goal. In learning to lead, however, I discovered that if I didn't have a vision on what I wanted my organization to look like, it was difficult to get employees juiced and jazzed on accomplishing it.

Michael Hyatt, former President and CEO of Thomas Nelson Publishers, author of *Platform: Get Noticed in a Noisy World*, and one of the top bloggers and speakers in the world, says "vision and strategy are both important. But there is a priority to them. Vision always comes first. Always. If you have a clear vision, you will eventually attract the right strategy. If you don't have a clear vision, no strategy will ever save you." He tells the story about taking over Nelson Books, a division of Thomas Nelson Publishers, and realizing it was in dire straits financially—much worse than he thought. The first thing he did? Developed a clear vision on what he wanted it to look like in three years, and developed a vision that he found compelling, and gave it to his employees. At this point, he didn't worry about the "how"—and he says getting stuck in the "how" too early keeps you off track to the "what." He did turn it around, not in three years, but in 18 months. That's how effective a compelling vision can be.[9]

To be honest, most of the "vision" exercises I've been through in organizations were pretty bland. It was usually something we were told to do, and coming up with pretty words that pleased the boss was the point. I don't remember ever being asked if it "moved" us.

That's not what it's supposed to be, however. It's supposed to be a picture of the future that inspires commitment. The end result should say, "Here is where we are headed, who is involved (show them how they fit in), what we are going to accomplish, and this is why we are doing this." In addition to a picture of what the future looks like, with words that make it compelling *to them*, it encourages your team to come up with creative and innovative ideas for accomplishment.

If you give them a reason for why they are there, get them on board and encourage them, you can stand back and watch how much they will accomplish—far more than you can do by yourself. A shared vision also bonds your team together in commitment when projects get off track—and serves as the azimuth for getting back on it.

Think of Martin Luther King's "I have a dream" speech.

President John F. Kennedy's vision and speech to Congress in January of 1961 to go to the moon by the end of the decade.

Henry Ford's vision where every family had an automobile.

These were all compelling visions, way before any of that happened or anyone knew "how."

How about this one? Krispy Kreme Donuts' mission—prominently displayed on their website: "Our vision is to be the worldwide leader in sharing delicious tastes and creating joyful memories." Not as lofty, but just as meaningful and attractive to those hearing it!

As busy leaders, it's still well worth the time to sit down and really think through where your organization is headed. This can give you clarity that will help you assign work, decide how and which projects to select, how many resources to devote to each one, and when they are no longer needed. I have even seen leaders who, after doing some vision planning, became aware that their team wasn't integral to the overall accomplishment of the organization's purpose, and were able to take on other projects so they wouldn't become obsolete.

As a minimum, you will want to think about:

- What is the purpose of my organization, and how would it affect this industry or agency if it no longer existed?

- What are we doing that's distinctive, or what can we do better than anyone else?

- Where do I want to see our organization in three years in terms my company measures (i.e., revenue, revenue growth, new business, innovative technologies, etc.)

- Who all is involved in our business (who are our stakeholders, customers, employees, etc.)? Do I have a way to measure our engagement with each one?

- How will I get my team involved and excited about where I want to see our organization go and create the goals to make that happen?

- How can I model and live my vision consistently so that my employees know I am dedicated to achieving it?

Remember, your organization is a living thing that needs to be nurtured over time if it is to grow. Giving employees a shared vision keeps them engaged and creative. It gives them the confidence that you know where you are going and how they fit in. It makes them want to work for you and achieve greater results.

You can give them this. Remember, what your company sells won't move them—but as the leader, *you* can. Jack Welch said, "Good business leaders create a vision, articulate the vision, passionately own the vision, and relentlessly drive it to completion."

Communicate Clear Expectations

When you board a flight and get settled in for takeoff, the first thing the pilot (or the head of the flight crew) does is give you the welcome speech. You get the destination, flying time, the weather at the destination, and information on expected turbulence. You also get information on what to expect in terms of services, meals, and entertainment.

Although setting clear expectations may seem like an obvious way to motivate your team, I have been guilty of assuming my team knew my expectations when they didn't. In fact, I have seldom had employees fail me who knew exactly what I considered what a "success" looked like.

Take my client, Frank. Frank had recently transferred in from another location to supervise a team, and he was frustrated. His biggest challenge with this new team was that no one would take notes in meetings that involved other leaders and team members outside their area. His team would "hear" different things in the meeting. As a result, there were several misunderstandings over due dates, and whose responsibility it was for various parts of a project. It seemed like an easy-to-overcome problem, so I asked him, "What do they say when you've asked them to take notes and they don't?" Frank looked at me in shock. "I shouldn't have to tell them to do this; they should know," he said. When I asked him how they should know, he said it was because when he was coming up in the organization, it was an expectation, and "he always knew to do it."

I reminded Frank that since this was a new group for him, with a different culture and different supervisors (and perhaps different expectations) in the past, it was a possibility they had never been taught as he had. Furthermore, by setting the expectation he was not only pleasing himself, he was doing something to help them—they would learn to listen so that they could convey the right information to the entire group.

Upon his concern that no one person get stuck with the duty, I suggested he rotate the "note-taking" duty from meeting to meeting, and have that person responsible for recording and disseminating the minutes. That way, everyone could have a clear understanding about who was responsible for what, with the tasks that came out of the meeting and the due dates. Not only would they listen better, especially if they were the note-taker, but it would also be a fair distribution of work—everyone would get a turn. I also encouraged him to tell them why. When we are given a task and know why, we are able to put the importance of it in context. Many times, I have even had employees come up with a better idea than I had.

When I went to the U. S. Army War College for a one-year

program, I learned something called "commander's intent." The official military definition is that commander's intent "succinctly describes what constitutes success for the operation. It includes the operation's purpose, key tasks, and the conditions that define the end state. It links the mission, concept of operations, and tasks to subordinate units."

What this really means is when a military commander gives out a task, he or she says why it's important and what a successful end state looks like. I worked for a leader, a one-star general in the Pentagon, who was a master at this. He never told me how to do something, but he gave me his "commander's intent" and I knew exactly what he wanted, why it was important, and what a successful end state looked like.

Here is what you will want to ensure you cover:

- End State/Clear Success Criteria. A good way to do this is say, "This project will be successful if…" and articulate that. Let them know what the measurement will be, and be specific and descriptive.

- Why are we doing it?

- By when (completion date)?

- Who is involved?

- What are their roles and responsibilities?

- What are the interim reporting requirements or milestones and who is responsible for the report, and how?

- What is the level of authority your team has before they come to you?

- Are there any risks they need to know?

Now listen. Ask them to restate their understanding of the success criteria. Encourage questions. Restate and clarify. The meeting shouldn't end until you ensure everyone is clear. Ask for commitment. Ask for questions. Invite them to tell you pitfalls you may not have thought of. I have even seen successful leaders who ask the team leader to write down what they heard, and submit it to them, so they will ensure understanding.

By the way, setting expectations can be used by you to ensure you have everything you need when you are given a task by your boss. It's effective to manage your boss' expectations, especially when the resources you are given are not adequate for a project, and the management "layers" above you might not realize it. By laying out your answers to these questions, you can provide your leader with information on exactly what can be accomplished with the resources you have, and what could be accomplished with more, so that he or she can see it in understandable terms. That way, you aren't judged to be whining about "I don't have enough people." You have shown it in a way that looks rational and well thought-out.

For example, under "End State/Clear Success Criteria," after, "this project will be successful, " you state what you believe the success criteria is they want. Then: "With this much money and this many people and no overtime, we can deliver...," Or: "With the number of people and money available, we can deliver what you want by such-and-such date." It's a good, rational way to say, "You want it better, faster, and cheaper: pick two of those," without being seen as negative (and without saying that!). It's worked for me many times, and I invite you to try it.

I'm going to provide something that is, by itself, worth the price of this book. Through the kindness and permission of Richard Scherberger, owner of Executive Leadership Skills, International, it's the best model I've found to ensure you have covered what you need when you begin a project and set expectations. His company conducts leadership training all over the world, and some of his former students have told me they run their organizations by his model. It's called GRRREPPP©

GRRREPPP©

At one time or another, most organizations suffer from a malady called GRRREPPP. GRRREPPP occurs whenever there is ambiguity in, confusion about, or duplication in one or more of the following areas:

G-Goals: Are they realistic? Are they well defined? Are they attainable? Are they communicated, understood, and shared by all? What are the teams goals? What is the team's purpose and/or mission? How do the team's goals mesh with the organization's mission and goals?

R-Roles: What preconceived ideas are there about the roles of the various levels of the organization and the members within those levels? What is the difference between established roles vs. role-playing? How much rold ambiguity and role conflict exists?

R-Responsibilities: Are responsibilities for task accomplishment clear? Is there commensurate authority to carry out responsibilities?

R-Relationships: What are the relationships among peers? Between peers and other members of the organization? What are some examples of these relationships? How clear is the importance of the relationships? How are relationships maintained? Are the relationships relaxed or tense? How will relationships be formed and maintained within the team? How will relationships be managed with individuals and groups outside the team? How will the team find the time to both form relationships and work on the tasks it undertakes? How well do team members work together?

E-Expectations: What are the organizational expectations? How are they aligned? Does each individual know what is expected of them and in turn what they can expect from other organizational members/levels of the organization? Unfulfilled expectations are frequently the cause of most organizational stress.

P-Plans: What plans exist to achieve the goal? Is the organization flying by the seat of its pants? Do members depend on other members in the organization to determine courses of action?

P-Priorities: Does the organization prioritize its tasks? What are the priorities in the organization? What's most important? Does the organization's actions match its stated priorities? Who establishes what's important in the organization?

P-Procedures: How much of a strict adherence to procedures is there? Where's the emphasis: procedures or outcomes? To what extent are procedures used as a crutch?

When GRRREPPP is present, organizations are not working to their fullest potential and the disease is depleting organizational energy.

Communicate By Having More Effective Meetings

As busy leaders, there are few things harder to balance than time for meetings. They are both a necessity for communication and a time waster. Since meetings today are so much more convenient to schedule using calendar software, and easier for employees to attend with video teleconferencing and phone conferencing, our meeting time has exploded. One survey by Bain & Company, a management research firm, found that on average, senior executives spent more than two days every week in meetings involving three or more coworkers. They also say that 15% of an organization's collective time is spent in meetings—a percentage that has increased every year since 2008.

And those meetings are not always effective. Harvard Business Review author Michael C. Mankins said in an article that "our research reveals, as much as 80% of top management's time is devoted to issues that account for less than 20% of a company's long-term value."[10]

We want to be great communicators, and we want to be sure that we are giving all the information our team needs to be effective. Here are some recommendations I give my clients.

- Develop a written agenda and distribute it ahead of time.

- Decide ahead and make it clear on the agenda whether the meeting is for *information gathering or brainstorming*, such as a team meeting to decide on a recommendation, *information sharing*, such as a staff meeting, or a *decision meeting* where a decision will be made by the leader.

- Ensure the right people are at the meeting. Eliminate unnecessary attendees—have only those people who need to be there participate.

- Start and end on time. Start promptly when you say you will and stick to the agenda. If issues come up that need to be discussed, designate someone to work that issue for the next time, or if it's important, a separate decision meeting. If it's information that needs to be shared and it's lengthy, have that person designated to ensure everyone gets the information.

- Designate a recorder and have that person responsible for disseminating tasks, who is the responsible party, and due dates.

- Set the expectation up-front on whether or not you want deliberations shared outside the meeting.

- Develop a positive culture where everyone is invited to be honest, and if there is disagreement that takes too long, agree to table that discussion for later.

By the way, if most everyone in the meeting is checking their cell phones for texts, or their eyes glaze over, you probably either have the wrong people at the meeting, or your agenda isn't robust enough to keep everyone engaged. I know one leader who sets her meetings for half the time of a "normal" meeting, and bans cell phones in the room. I know another who has short stand-up meetings each morning to launch the day. It keeps everyone engaged and makes them shorter because they have to stand.

I've included some books in the Resources Section that I recommend to my clients. I invite you to try some of these techniques and see if your communications in meetings improve, including what worked for you and what didn't.

How Am I Doing At Saying What I Mean And Meaning What I Say?

1. Do I have a clear vision for where I want my organization to be in three years? One year?

2. Do my employees know what this vision is?

3. Have I ensured this vision fits in with what my boss wants our organization to look like so that I know my team is relevant?

4. Do I set expectations clearly so my employees know what I need, why I need it, when I need it, and any limitations they have?

5. Do I have a handle on meetings: how much time we are using? Is it productive? Are the right people there? Do attendees feel free to share in meetings?

CHAPTER 5
Step 4: Do You Hear What I'm Saying?

I remind myself every morning: Nothing I say this day will teach me anything. So if I'm going to learn, I must do it by listening.. – **Larry King**

Listening is the part of communicating that is so important that I thought it warranted its own chapter. Listening can make the difference between success and failure in an organization. It can be the difference between a healthy organization full of creative ideas and innovation, and an organization where information isn't shared and people are scrambling to leave. It can make a difference in profit and loss, and it can even be the difference in solving problems early or letting them fester until they become grievances, or even lawsuits.

The Merriam-Webster dictionary defines listening as: "to pay attention to someone or something in order to hear what is being said." So when we are not listening well, it means we are unable to separate what is being said from our own needs around the conversation.

When we think about good communication skills, sometimes we really just want to learn how to get our message across, and can skirt on the edge of wanting to manipulate the conversation so that we get what we want. But as leaders, we can't be effective by giving orders—our role is to engage our employees, our colleagues, and our customers. And listening is totally receiving. It's not manipulative, and it's not passive. It's not about us. It's probably the most important thing we do as leaders, because otherwise we never learn anything new.

About 90 percent of my clients tell me it's the skill they most need to get better at doing, and when I was leading an organization, it's the skill I struggled with the most. The listening we really are lacking, as leaders, is listening at a level that is more than the words being spoken—something called *deep listening.*

What Is Deep Listening?

Deep listening is a way of listening where we are fully present in the moment with the person who is speaking, and we are not trying to judge or control the conversation. We let go of our assumptions, to hear for what is *being said.* We are listening for the emotions, motives, needs and goals of the person who is speaking.

Have you been in a meeting where your mind wandered, and near the end you didn't remember most of what had been discussed? Or listening to a person giving you a status of a project, and you are thinking ahead on what you will say? I certainly have been guilty of this many times. I struggled with overcoming the urge to jump in and give an answer before the other person had even finished speaking. That was because rather than listening, I thought I already knew what they were going to say (and the answer) and wanted to move on to something else. So many times when people have been talking, I realized I was thinking, "How does this affect me?" Or, "What can I say next to convince her I'm right?" Or even, "I wish he'd shut up so we can finish this meeting." As Mark Twain once said, "There is nothing so annoying as having two people talking when you're busy interrupting."

When we are poor listeners, we interrupt, jump to conclusions about what the other person is going to say, or we tune it out. I have even been guilty of waiting for the other person to "take a breath" (if they have been talking for some time), so I can jump in! Obviously, I am not listening to another opinion when this happens! Deep listening is an acquired skill that does take some self-discipline and practice, but it's the only way we are likely to find out what's really going on in the organization.

A story was told about Franklin Roosevelt, who often endured long receiving lines at the White House. He complained that no one really paid any attention to what was said. One day, during a reception, he decided to try an experiment. When each person passed down the line and shook his hand, he murmured, "I murdered my grandmother this morning." The guests responded with phrases like, "Marvelous! Keep up the good work. We are proud of you. God bless you, sir." It was not till the end of the line, while greeting the ambassador from Bolivia, that his words were actually heard. Nonplussed, the ambassador leaned over and whispered, "I'm sure she had it coming." (Source unknown.)

Why Should We Care?

So why develop this skill? It's the only way we are going to learn what's going on with our team. Listening:

69

- Is the foundation for making a personal connection with your employees

- Builds trust and respect

- Lets you understand other people's point of view

- Encourages the sharing of information you need to make good decisions

- Reduces tensions and conflict

- Makes it more likely that the other person will listen to us

- Creates a safe environment for collaboration and feedback

By learning to be a great listener, we can be the kind of leader who transforms organizations, that everyone wants to work for, and the kind of leader that makes others want to hire us.

I worked for a general officer in the Army who said the worst thing a leader can do is be surprised by his boss, who already had information he should have known and didn't. He wanted to be sure we always gave him the information we had. Getting honest and open feedback on what is going on with your team, and what might go wrong—then dealing with those up front—could make all the difference in being able to execute a good idea you have or failing. Your team is not going to give you this feedback, however, if you have a history of either not listening or discounting what they say.

When we have a reputation for not listening we become like Bill, a leader I worked for. Bill was the Director of the organization, and was excited about his new initiative. Sure, it was going to require changing a few systems and doing some things differently, but this was really going to impress the corporate office.

He laid it out in the morning's executive staff meeting, telling the team how and when it would be done.

Some of the executive team looked down at their phones while he was talking. A few of them nodded and smiled politely. They had all discussed this initiative before, and had told Bill what the challenges would be.

He didn't ask for recommendations on what issues they thought they might encounter to make the initiative work. Nor did he ask if his timeline made sense.

I knew what they were thinking.

Jan, Head of IT, was thinking about the myriad of systems this project would involve and how much time it would take—and what about the other two high-priority projects that corporate headquarters had going? Her staff was already working overtime.

Ben, the CFO, was remembering last week's meeting where Bill said they had to cut costs this year. Seems revenue wasn't keeping up with the costs of corporate's new initiatives.

Gail in Operations was worried about the building renovation. Every time they were close to a design, Bill thought of something else to add, including that new marble foyer right outside his office.

The Nodders and Phone Checkers had long since given up

asking questions about priorities and cost benefits, or giving suggestions. The last time one of them tried that, Bill put them in their place, even accused them of being "negative" and "not strategic."

To make a long story short, we did start that initiative. Several months and lots of (spent) money later, we had made little progress and had lots of challenges. The project had to be abandoned when Bill had to explain his lack of progress on other projects at a corporate meeting. Most of these problems—and delays—could have been anticipated and avoided, and Bill might have been a hero, if he had been the kind of leader whose team felt free to ask probing questions and give negative feedback on his ideas. *If he showed them he was the kind of leader who listened.*

Specifically, Bill could have presented his idea with an open mind. For example: "I'm excited about this idea; therefore, I'm not likely to see the pitfalls in relation to what else we have going on. I want to capture what these may be before we make any decisions about how to move forward. I'm listening."

And meant it. But if we, like Bill, have squelched our team's ideas before, especially publicly, and refused to listen, it's going to take awhile before they will trust us enough to give an analysis of those ideas.

William Ury, co-author of *Getting to Yes: Negotiating Agreement Without Giving In*, gave a TED Talk where he said he believed listening was the lost "other half" of communication. He told a story about being called as a consultant to the President of Venezuela, President Chavez, during the time of his opposition. President Chavez was extremely upset over the rebellion and yelled about the situation for half an hour. Ury said he just listened, and finally, Chavez stopped, his shoulders sagging, and said, "What should I do?" Ury said at that time, the entire mood changed in the room—because those words were the sound of a mind opening—he was ready to listen.

A more famous example was NASA's Columbia Disaster, when the space shuttle exploded and killed all the astronauts on board. I began working at NASA shortly after it occurred on February 1, 2003, as we scrutinized ourselves and our organizational failures, one of them being "...organizational barriers that prevented effective communication of critical safety information and stifled professional differences of opinion..."[11] In a nutshell: engineers tried to bring up the issue, and were not listened to.

Why We Don't Do It Well

If learning to listen well is so important, why don't we do it better? Because it's not easy! In fact, there are many barriers that can make us poor listeners that we might not recognize in ourselves:

- We'd rather talk.

- We're busy and frustrated over being "bothered."

- We're distracted.

- We're bored with the subject or it's too complex.

- We don't believe we will learn anything.

- We're biased toward the speaker.

- We are waiting for them to finish, and formulating a response for when they do (called "fake listening").

- We have trouble accepting new ideas, criticism, and other feedback.

- We're tired.

Actually, when it comes to listening, introverted leaders seem to have the edge on the extraverts. I love Dilbert comics by Scott Adams. One of them showed Doobert talking to Dilbert in the first frame. "I've decided to escalate my anti-social behavior from not listening to actively talking over other people," said Doobert.

Then both of them begin talking over each other. Dilbert says, "How can you enjoy the conversation of others if you don't listen," while Doobert's conversation overlays it and he says, "This could be one of the best ideas I've ever had."

Doobert then says, "It all came together when I realized that listening isn't the fun part."

It isn't always fun to be the listener. We have good intentions, but the day gets busy, there's a lot of noise and distractions, our calendars are full, and unexpected things happen. Taking time out to have those conversations and put in the energy to listen to our employees gets pushed aside. As Stephen R. Covey, the author of *The 7 Habits of Highly Effective People* said, "Most people do not listen with the intent to understand; they listen with the intent to reply."

How We Can Do It Better

I realize that listening takes time and we are already busy. But without it, we just can't inspire, transform or motivate our team. Here are some ways I've found—many of them shared from other leaders—about how to do it better. By the way, this works with colleagues and bosses too.

- *Listen to yourself first.* William Ury recommends we do this every time we have a conversation where we need to listen: take a few minutes, get quiet and listen to yourself. Take some time to get the flurry of thoughts out of your head, even if you have to write them down in a to-do list and put them aside for later. That way, you aren't thinking of all those things when you are trying to listen. Then ask yourself: "What is my intention that I want to come away with from the conversation?" and listen to yourself. What are your motives? What is the best result that can come from your conversation for all parties? This also works well before meetings, and it can help gather your thoughts about what you want to know by the end of the meeting.

- *Schedule time.* Set aside time on your calendar with the person you are having the conversation with and close the door against interruptions. Deep listening takes time and you can't do it with distractions.

- *Be sincere and open.* In order to listen well, we must be willing to let the other person dominate the discussion while we tune in. Being open minded to another opinion, even though it disagrees with our own, and genuinely interested in what the other person has to say, is the only way we will learn anything new.

- *Tune in.* Hearing every word someone says is not necessarily listening. Deep listening is not only hearing the *content* of what the other person is saying, but the *context*—where the other person is "coming from"—what's the purpose of them saying it; why are they telling you this—what needs are motivating them? Deep listening to someone else encourages them to feel heard and speak more openly and honestly. Although you may be gathering facts, there is seldom "the truth"—and if you rant out of anger and make them wrong, you may stifle the conversation before it gets started. Listen with intention. Then listen again. *What do they really want?* It's OK to ask that question!

- *Appreciate their point of view.* Don't let their position in the company influence how you listen. Every person in an organization has something to contribute. We often find out information that we need from people who we think are least likely to have it. I've found that even if I don't agree with the other person's point of view, it's vital to understand it. How else can you work through a solution?

- *Clarify if you don't understand.* Take care not to interrupt, but when your employee gets to a "stopping place" in the conversation, ask open-ended questions to clarify and reflect back the substance and feelings you heard. Then ask for clarification and listen again.

- *Be aware of your body language.* It sometimes speaks much louder than we do. Our employees can tell when we can't wait for them to finish. If we lean back and distance ourselves with our arms crossed like we are uninterested, they won't open up, and we won't get to find out what they want to tell us. Lean toward them or take a neutral body position, and give them your undivided attention. Remember, we are listening for the feelings and real reasons they have come to us, not just the words.

What if someone comes to you and you really don't have the time to listen well? Maybe you are on your way to a meeting in a few minutes, or have something you really must finish? Ask them to come back if possible. For example, "I have a meeting in 10 minutes; however, I want to give you the time you need, and I know what we need to talk about is important. If you can come back at 2:45, I can give you the time we will need."

It takes skill, and it also takes *courage: courage to put ourselves in a receiving position, courage to be open and vulnerable, and sometimes hear what we may not want to.* Winston Churchill was renowned for his ability to sit down and listen to everyone and this statement is attributed to him: "Courage is what it takes to stand up and speak; courage is also what it takes to sit down and listen."

Learning to listen can change our work life. Jim Hough, a friend who has been a marketing and creative professional for over 30 years, says learning to listen has become the *most* valuable skill when it comes to doing his job well. Here's what he told me: "The creative process is all about collaboration and getting people to engage with each other to find a solution—a better, newer, unconventional solution. Nearly 20 years ago, I stumbled upon Steven Covey's *7 Habits of Highly Effective People* and it changed my life and work. Habit 5 is, "Seek first to understand, then to be understood." Those eight words turned my world upside down. Up to that point, I thought, as a leader, it was my job to communicate my ideas, my desires, and my expectations so those I lead would be clear about how they were to spend their time and effort. I spent much more time talking than listening. The flow of information was, for the most part, one way…from me to them. As a result, I rarely got helpful suggestions or ideas from my team. They became doers, but not thinkers. But I wanted thinkers…and I was confused as to why I wasn't able to nurture that in others."

Once I discovered Habit 5, I realized how very wrong I was about communication and collaboration. It finally dawned on me that communication was not making sure I got *my* point across, but giving others a forum to express *their* thoughts— *first*, before I try to express my own thoughts. Once I began to do this with my employees (not to mention my wife and kids) there was skepticism at first, but then, people opened up. They began to feel safe, over time, to share their thoughts more and more. I was shocked at how quickly I was surrounded by thinkers instead of just doers. My job became much easier, and our collective work became much better and more effective.

Jim says the key is that there is nothing more important to a person than to feel heard and understood. "Covey calls it "emotional oxygen," he said. "Once we feel that we've been heard, we're open and willing to hear another opinion. I have as much freedom to express my ideas as I ever have, but now, I choose to wait until the other person talks. And more times than not, fully hearing their perspective changes and informs my own thoughts."

Deep listening as part of communication is a rare and wonderful thing! It's worth the effort and discipline of seeking to understand, first, then to be understood.

When we deeply listen as leaders, we are showing up for our people and being exactly the kind of leader that makes a positive difference in our organization. When our employees believe we are really listening to them, they believe we trust in their goals for the conversation, have an open mind, and want the highest and best intention for them. If we are the kind of leader who listens, our team will come to us while we can still deal with challenges. We won't get any unwelcome surprises of information that we needed earlier. They will ensure we know what we need to ensure success.

People want to know you really hear them. Brendon Burchard said, "All of us want someone to care who we are and what we think and feel. That's why we all should see everyone in the world as having a sign hung around his neck that reads, 'Please listen to me and value me.'"

How Am I Doing As A Listening Leader?

How well would my employees and colleagues say I listen?

1. Do I take time to listen to myself before a conversation and before meetings, so that I can then concentrate on the speaker?

2. Do I schedule time and put away distractions for meetings with colleagues and employees?

3. Am I sincere and open with the conversation? Do I really want to know how they feel and do I want new information? Do I really want a different point of view?

4. Do I tune in to the context of the conversation as well as the content?

5. Do I interrupt colleagues and employees while they are talking, or am I thinking about what to say before they finish?

6. Do I clarify after the conversation to ensure I've heard them?

7. Is my body language open? Do I avoid looking frustrated or "closed"?

CHAPTER 6
Step 5: Praise and Feedback

Employees who report receiving recognition and praise within the last seven days show increased productivity, get higher scores from customers, and have better safety records. They're just more engaged at work. – **Tom Rath, author of *Strengthsfinder 2.0***

We all need people who will give us feedback. That's how we improve. – **Bill Gates**

Mastering the skills of giving praise and giving great feedback is going to be like icing on the cake. You already have the foundation, and this is just going to make you more confident and help your team perform better.

Let's talk about what praise is, how and when to give it, and how to do it sincerely. When we talk feedback, we are going to talk about how to make it effective, but also how to give the feedback that most leaders dread: when things aren't going well and need to improve.

Giving Praise

Think about a boss you worked for and didn't like. How often did he or she say "thank you" when you did something well? How about giving you credit in front of others for projects you completed on time, or problems you recognized that saved the team time or money? On a scale of 1 to 10, how would they rate? I'll bet it was pretty low.

If you remember a boss who didn't give you praise, or you don't get much now, you are not alone. According to the Gallup Business Journal, their survey reported that fewer than one in three American workers said that they received praise from their supervisor within the last seven days. They also reported that "the instances where employees received 'recognition or praise for doing good work' was responsible for a 10-20 percent difference in revenue and productivity."[12] And remember, you can thank someone in ten or fifteen seconds—a very cheap way to improve your bottom line!

When I say "praise" I just mean a heart-felt "thank you for doing a good job on that." It doesn't have to be money, and it doesn't have to cost time or effort. Notice that the survey said "in the last seven days?" That might seem like a short time-frame; however, their research suggests that we react much better to shorter-term rewards like a pat on the back, rather than a big awards celebration at the end of the year.

As leaders, we find ourselves going through our day looking for something wrong. After all, that's what we get paid for, right? To find things that are going wrong and need to be fixed before it gets costly? It's hard to find time to look for something going right, and give proper credit to the person making that happen, but that's also the leader's job. Especially when it can make such a positive difference in productivity.

Why Give Praise?

Everyone loves appreciation. They love to be told "thank you," especially when they have just solved a problem, or finished some project that's important to the company. They even love a "thank you for all you do" comment, especially from their leaders. It's well-documented that people who feel appreciated and respected for their work are more motivated to work harder and perform better than when their efforts go unnoticed. Why? Research tells us it's the neurotransmitter, dopamine, which causes this sensation in our brains when we are being appreciated.

Dopamine is the chemical transmitter the brain generates that causes a feeling of joy, well-being, equilibrium and satisfaction in the body. It's the same substance that gets turned on with all sorts of pleasures, like food and exercise, and for some people, gambling and shopping. And we can turn it on with appreciation and praise! Praising your employees not only makes them feel great, it makes you feel good, too. And it makes them want to experience that same feeling again (the brain connection), so they want to continue the good work.

Giving praise and appreciation also helps develop good relationships with colleagues, and makes them more likely to return the feelings. Not only does this make for better working relationships, but it is also much more likely they will provide help when you need it, or share information they could just as well withhold for themselves.

What is praise and appreciation? It can be formal recognition, such as an award. Examples are a company's President's Award, Employee of the Month, or Salesman of the Year. These are typically widely publicized throughout the company, and may or may not come with a monetary bonus, time off, a trip, or a medal. Or it can be informal, such as a sincere, personal "thank you" to a person for something they've done, in person, email, or a handwritten note, or a verbal recognition or thank you in front of others.

I've had numerous discussions with clients on how they are rewarding their employees, and an answer I frequently get is, "We are under a tight budget this year," and "We don't have any bonus money this year." When I ask them about other forms of recognition, and how often they do an informal "thank you" to an employee in front of others, it surprises me that I get a look of surprise myself.

Let me tell you about a difference it made to Tonya. Here's her story as she told it to me:

"I facilitated our team meeting (30-35 people) on our Myers-Briggs Type Indicator results. Everyone there works in my organization or supports it in some way, such as being matrixed from other organizations, or as direct support, like I am. However, we didn't all know each other very well, and some people did not know each other at all. As we discussed everyone's indicators and what they meant, we also discussed the strengths and weakness of each indicator. I'm ESFJ (Extrovert, Sensing, Feeling, Judging), by the way. As we began to talk, someone remarked that they noticed I had improved my need to show appreciation to people after I attended a workshop with them in a previous organization.

There was a reason for that. At the previous workshop, which lasted three days, when we discussed the importance of appreciation, I started to tune out. Frankly, I hadn't seen the importance of showing appreciation. My philosophy was, "Everyone gets paid to do their job and that should be enough."

On the other hand, I strongly desired appreciation for myself. I need reassurance, "atta boys," back pattings, validation, etc. It was ridiculous that what I craved for myself, I didn't see as important enough to give out to others. I suddenly realized that not only did I need it, but if I didn't get it, I went looking for it.

At that point, our manager, Bob, stood up and said he had been to a workshop a few years prior and had really begun to understand the importance of showing employees appreciation. He said he would like to take that opportunity and show everyone there what they meant to him.

Bob started at the front of the room and stood in front of that first gentlemen, looked him straight in the eye, and told him specific, detailed things he did in his job that made Bob appreciate him.

By the third employee, Bob had tears in his eyes, and they rolled down his cheeks the remainder of the time, as he told each of us, one by one, what our work meant to him and how it made his job easier. Each person's appreciation statement was personal and different. It wasn't just a shallow thank you. It wasn't something he prepared ahead of time. It was something from the heart. And as Bob continued, everyone was moved and most were moved to tears.

I was fourth from last. When he got to me, I was crying so much I could barely see him. He told me several things, but one thing that stands out and I will never forget: He told me that although I supported over 100 people, that every time I supported him with an action, I made him feel like he was the only person on my agenda that day, and that I made him feel special.

After Bob finished with everyone in the room, there were only sounds of crying and clapping as we were so moved by his outpouring of emotion over all of our service to him. No one could speak. That was the day I realized the power of appreciation. There is absolutely nothing I wouldn't do to help out Bob. I told him that day that no matter what position I obtain in that organization or any other, and no matter what awards I receive, nothing will ever mean as much to me as what he did that day. I will hold that moment in my heart forever and I will never forget the power of appreciation and the impact it has on people.

I changed how I thought about people that day. It was no longer just about getting a job done the most effective, efficient way. Sure that's important, but it's the people that are really what's important. If you take care of the people and show them you appreciate the great work they do, they will continue to strive to give you better and better work, and you'll achieve getting the job done the most effective, efficient way because the employee wants you to be proud of them. They want you to show it in a real way—not just a casual "thank you" while passing by them in the hallway. Appreciation has to be from the heart and done consistently."

How We Can Do Better

Praise and appreciation has to be sincere. Just as you can, your employees and colleagues can spot manipulation every time. If you never say "thank you," and suddenly you say it and then ask for someone to work overtime, they are probably not going to be fooled. If you don't mean it—just don't say it.

A sincere appreciation *with their name* along with it makes them more productive, but at the very least makes for a better day. Dr. Vicky Scherberger, Director of Consulting and Training, Executive Leadership Skills, International, always says, "The sweetest sound a person hears is the sound of their own name." No matter how big a group she has, her goal on the first day of one of her training classes is to learn and call each person by name.

Imagine you are hearing this from your boss: "Good job on catching that budget problem." Pretty good, right? Now, what if he or she said: "Great job, Paul. You really nailed that budget problem. If you hadn't caught that error, our whole project may have been behind schedule." Can you see the difference?

Never underestimate the value of a handwritten note or an email, but especially effective is a sincere, "Thank you for doing a great job, Paul," in front of Paul's team of colleagues.

I have had leaders who told me that people were just doing what they paid them to do, and thanks shouldn't be necessary. Maybe it shouldn't. But think again on how much effort you often put into projects that your boss doesn't see—he or she just sees the results—and how rewarding it would be to get a "thank you" for doing so.

A word of caution here: don't praise someone if they don't deserve it. Telling them they have done a good job if they haven't is worse than no praise at all. I challenge you, however, to find something to thank every employee for every now and then, and if they do absolutely nothing you can thank them for, why are they working for you? Sometimes when leaders are going through difficulties with an employee, a little thanks on their efforts makes a world of difference.

If you can't think of things to thank people for, try some of these:

- Their integrity

- Their willingness to take a risk

- Their ability to help solve customers' problems

- Their willingness to work cooperatively with their team

- Their great attitude

- Their teaching of new employees

- Their loyalty to you

- Their dedication

- Their ideas

- Their professionalism

Get the idea? Nothing you do to make your team better costs as little and gives such a great reward. Dr. Bob Nelson, president of Nelson Motivation Inc., motivational speaker and author of *1001 Ways to Reward Employees*, now in a new edition entitled *1501 Ways to Reward Employees*, says, "Systematically start to thank your employees when they do good work whether it's one-on-one in person, in the hallway, in a group meeting, on voicemail, in a written thank-you note, on email or at the end of each day at work. Better yet, go out of your way to act on and share and amplify good news when it occurs—even if it means interrupting someone to thank them for a great job they have done. By taking the time to say you noticed and appreciate their efforts, those efforts—and results—will continue."

Dr. Nelson says the trends affecting the workplace today make it even more important. Trends such as more use of technology (few "high touch" experiences with our leaders), the need for employees to find more meaning in their jobs (Gen Xers and Millenials), and the need for employees to take more initiative in their jobs makes appreciation and praise even more important. And in a tightly controlled economic environment, it's a great, low-cost way to improve employee performance as well.

As leaders we need to remember a famous quote by Mary Kay Ash, founder of Mary Kay Cosmetics, when she said: "There are two things people want more than sex and money: recognition and praise."

Giving Feedback

What do employees want more than your praise? Your honest feedback, if it's done in a constructive manner. In a Harvard Business Review survey in January of 2014, employees said feedback did more to improve their performance than praise.[13] When we think of giving feedback, we often think of counseling employees when something is going wrong. Nothing could be further from reality. As we start to learn new things, or take on new tasks, we need feedback from those who already know what success looks like in order to get back on course.

For example, automated flight control systems have a feedback loop to stay on course. The pilot sets a control mode to maintain the wings in a level position. Even with the smoothest air, the wings will dip. Position sensors on the wing then detect this and send a signal to the autopilot computer, which sends a signal to the servos that control the aircraft's ailerons. The servo has an electric motor fitted with a clutch, that goes through a bridle cable, grips the aileron cable and when the cable moves, the control surfaces move and the ailerons are adjusted back toward level. The autopilot computer removes the command when the position sensor says the wing is level. This is a feedback loop that works many times during flight without human intervention.

Sometimes we want to have a feedback loop, we know we need one, but we aren't working with machines and we have to set it up. While we may have management control systems that show employees when something is out of kilter, most often our feedback is the only way our employees know what's working well and what isn't.

Of course we would all rather give positive feedback, but even when we can't we can give feedback in a *positive and constructive manner.*

In 2009, Gallup, Inc., conducted a study of over 1,000 employees in the United States and asked employees to rate their managers on whether or not they focused on strengths or positive characteristics, or weaknesses and negative characteristics, when giving feedback. The study pointed out that a manager's feedback style had a huge impact on how engaged or disengaged a direct report was likely to be. The survey showed that one in 10 supervisors focused on the weaknesses, and that employees who received predominantly negative feedback were over 20 times more likely to be engaged than if they were ignored or didn't receive any feedback. The managers who focused on strengths when giving feedback, however, were 30 times more likely to have actively engaged employees. But the survey also revealed that giving little or no feedback was worse than focusing on negative characteristics: *worse than giving people a negative comment is to ignore them and give them no feedback.*[14] People would rather be criticized than ignored altogether.

There is some research that suggests that occasionally, negative feedback, delivered the right way, can also improve performance. There is also research that indicates negative feedback is many more times likely to have significant adverse effects on an employee's productivity. I believe there can be occasions where negative feedback is warranted but must be delivered appropriately (read that *privately*!) and after you've exhausted other methods.

So Why Don't We Give Feedback?

One of the comments I hear from executives is, "I wish people would give me more feedback about how I can improve." Yet when it comes to leaders giving feedback to their team, it's often difficult, and seldom do I find a leader who is comfortable with it.

What they say is: "I don't have time." "If I give honest feedback, it will make an unhappy team." Or, "If I give honest feedback, nothing will change. Those people won't do anything differently."

What they mean is: "I don't want to be the bad guy," and "I really don't know how to do it in a positive way."

I had a leader in the Pentagon who was very unhappy with another employee. This was a tough guy, a General in the Army, but she was a civilian, and he just didn't know how to talk with her about it. Although he knew just how to relate to another military person when he was not happy with their work, and had no hesitation in doing so, he didn't have that comfort in dealing with a civilian. When he asked for my advice, I asked him what he had already said to her. It became obvious that when he didn't get something the way he had asked for it, he told her in such an indirect way that she never knew where her error was. As a civilian myself, I told him there was no way she could possibly know she was not meeting standards by the kind of feedback he gave her.

Sometimes it's difficult to be sincere but firm. Kind but direct. But we aren't helping our employees when we just want to be a people pleaser.

Your employees want this. The Harvard Business Review Survey mentioned above said that *by roughly a three to one margin*, they believe it does even more to improve their performance than praise.

How We Can Do Better

Learning to give good feedback is a skill that all leaders can master. It takes a desire and it takes practice. There's a ton of information on giving feedback, including books and articles on the subject. You can ask another leader who is a colleague, and good at it, to help you, or you can get a coach to help you.

Planning ahead for a feedback meeting and what your

intentions are for the results will help you get clear on what you want to say. It also helps you be more comfortable so that you can ensure your body language is open and welcoming, rather than stressed and irritated. Here are a few things that may help:

Give feedback often and appropriately. Every person who works for you is different. Some employees are highly skilled at their jobs and highly motivated. All they need is autonomy and a recognition that you realize they are doing a good job. In those cases, feedback is give-and-take discussion, centered around how the work is going, if there is anything they need from you, and how you can facilitate and support them. On the other end of the spectrum are newer, less-trained employees who need more experience and skills, and they may be highly motivated or not. They need more feedback so they know what they are doing well, and what they need to improve. And there is every kind of employee in between. Our job as leaders is to know which employee is which.

Make it regular. Regardless of your company's performance appraisal system, giving feedback does not mean waiting until official performance review time to let an employee know how he or she is doing. You will want to have some regular feedback meetings, and sometimes you will need to do them when specific issues come up. But no matter how busy you are, they should be as frequent as they need to be, depending on the employee's skill, experience, and the complexity of your on-going projects. Above all, *no employee should ever be surprised or get unexpected news when it comes time for a formal performance appraisal.* Never.

Make it private, make it specific, make it safe, and make it positive. Most of the feedback you give where you want to talk about improvements will be in private. An exception would be a small team meeting where you might use the "3 Ups and 3 Downs" method in Chapter 3. You want to give information related to their work goals. For example, *what* is the work goal, *how* are they doing toward the goal, *what's next* on the work goal, and *what actions* should be taken to make further progress on the goal? To make sure it's meaningful and helpful, focus on what you have observed around on-the-job behaviors, results, and teamwork. Be descriptive, not evaluative—things aren't "good" or "bad"—they are either meeting standards and on track with milestones or they aren't.

Employees will resent it if you give them feedback and they don't think you know anything about what they've been doing. If you aren't able to observe their performance first-hand, then be sure you tell them why you are giving them feedback (i.e., their team lead gave you his/her assessment, the project information they provided was exceptional or needs a little more work, etc.) If most of this is about good work, it makes for an easy meeting. One thing I've used that has worked well is to call them "learning meetings." When you tell employees you are going to have a "learning meeting," and they know this means, "We are going to talk about how things are going with your project, what's going well, and discuss where you need me to help facilitate improvement," they go into it with no defensiveness and a completely different attitude than if they believe they are being called on the carpet.

Get feedback. Before moving to problem solving, be sure to ask them how they believe they are doing and what else they need from you to improve. Ask them what they believed your expectations were. Often, clarifying expectations is all that is needed to ensure employee success. Give them a chance to talk about their own performance, and ask them what they learned. It's informative to hear their thoughts about how they were successful, or why they got the results that they did.

Most employees want to do a great job for you. They want you to notice their efforts and they want to know how to improve so they can advance in their careers, too. With a regular, positive, and constructive feedback loop, they can do just that.

As a leader, I would invite you to have someone you trust who can also give you honest feedback. I personally believe that we should have a mechanism in our performance reviews where we get peer feedback. One good way to do that is a 360-degree assessment, perhaps yearly. These are strictly confidential and can give you and your team a feedback loop with each other.

When It's A Difficult Conversation And Things Must Improve

It's the conversation every leader dreads. I know I do. Performance or behavior isn't up to the minimum standard and you have to talk with the employee. When you have to have one of these conversations, it's even more important to plan it ahead of time. Remember to get all your other distractions, thoughts, and emotions, especially if they are negative or angry, down on paper so you won't be tempted to use them in the meeting. And it's important to do it sooner, rather than later. These discussions delivered as close to the issue that needs addressing are the most effective. You will want to discuss:

- What's the specific behavior or performance you must address?

- What do you want? What is the highest and best result you want out of the conversation?

- Do you have all the facts about the situation, or do you need to gather other facts before the discussion?

- Is there anything you are pretending not to know about your role in the problem?

- Keep the discussion on how you feel about the work and/or behavior against a standard or work goal.

- Ask for clarification from them on their expectations around the work goal or behavior.

- Listen for their viewpoint without interrupting.

- Plan for the next step. In the meeting, you might make it their responsibility to come back to you with a plan for improvement and give them time to do that. If it has progressed past that point (this is not their first warning), you may have to do a plan for improvement. If so, you need to tell them so and when to expect it.

I've done this with success, and I've done it without success, and it's always better when you can turn an employee around. A friend of mine saw it happen first-hand in her office and she told me this story:

"I can count on one hand the number of times I have seen a manager turn an employee's poor performance completely around. Although it's extremely difficult and time consuming, it's an amazing thing to witness when it happens. My boss in the organization was Jim. Jim supervised several analysts, administrative officers, and several other people who didn't fit into an engineering-type role.

When Jim took over, his manager told him his organization had two "bad apples" in the batch. They were fine people, but they didn't perform to meet expectations. One of them was an engineer who had not been successful in his engineering role, and was placed into an analyst position at a much lower level than his skills and salary would warrant. In addition, the employee had absolutely no knowledge of anything the analysts did. Even though the employee was performing what you might consider a less-skilled job than an engineer, he couldn't perform as expected.

Instead of ignoring him, Jim worked tirelessly with this employee. His number one attribute in this process was patience. The employee lacked knowledge that an employee would have after working at this organization for a few months, yet Jim patiently taught him what he didn't know. Jim was astonished that managers had promoted this employee throughout the years given his lack of knowledge, skills, and desire to perform.

At the first performance interim appraisal time, Jim typed out everything very clearly for the employee on what was lacking, and discussed steps for how he could correct his performance. At first, the employee was resistant that Jim was correct in his assessment—he had apparently never been told by anyone in management that he was lacking in his performance, but finally realized that Jim was proceeding with a poor rating if he didn't improve. The employee slowly began to ask questions of Jim on how he could do better. Jim had such patience and showed him appreciation for every baby step he made along the way. I saw that employee ask questions in staff meetings that were ridiculous to me, yet Jim never rolled his eyes or insulted the employee. He always answered his questions patiently each time. I was so impressed by his ability to move slowly and patiently with this employee. And I saw him participate more in discussions, and he started to understand things better.

Within 18 months, I saw Jim take the employee, who had been written off by everyone else, and make him a productive member of this organization. This was six years ago, and he is still achieving quality results. He may never be the superstar employee but he succeeds in his job—something he was never made to do.

Jim believed in him. He had many one-on-one discussions with this employee and he told him he knew he could do the work. He knew he could achieve the goals they had and because Jim believed in him, he began to believe in himself."

How Am I Doing On Praise And Feedback?

1. How often do I give praise and "thank you's"?

    a. Is it part of my regular, daily routine as a leader?

    b. Is it sincere and do I call the person by name?

    c. Do i give informal appreciation, not just formal appreciation? Do I use a variety of ways to do that?

2. Have I mastered the skill of giving effective, positive, and meaningful feedback?

    a. Do I give it often and appropriately?

    b. Do I make it about the work goals?

    c. Do I do it in private, unless it's appropriate for a team meeting?

    d. Do I make it safe for employees? Do I make it a "learning" meeting rather than a "butt chewing"? Do I keep it positive?

    e. Do I give them a chance to clarify their expectations of me?

    f. Do I problem solve with my employees?

    g. Do I ensure we have a plan for improvement?

3. What about difficult situations where the employee's work or actions must change?

    a. Have I planned the meeting and ensured my emotions are out of the picture?

    b. Do I know what I want as a result?

    c. Do I ensure we have a plan for improvement or the next step?

CHAPTER 7
Commitment or Compliance?

Yours is not the only truth–everyone has their own.
–Richard Scherberger

You can always get someone to do what you want them to do—if they work for you and want to keep their job. In the short term.

Remember my employee, Rosslyn, in Chapter 1—who did a great presentation and was told by the Assistant Vice President that she had better not make a mistake or her career was over? Our boss had the positional power to get her *compliance*. And she got it. What she didn't have—and none of us do—is the power to get her *commitment*.

While for poor leaders compliance is enough, it isn't for the great ones. When employees are committed, they give themselves emotionally and intellectually to what they value—to you as a leader and to their job or project. It's a choice, and it's sustained by dedication and perseverance when challenges come along. Committed is being *intrinsically* motivated to do a job, which means we do it because it is enjoyable, and not for the reward.

An example of commitment is a story told at NASA back during the time when their rocket scientists were working hard to get to the moon, about an engineer who was so dedicated he slept at the office most nights. One morning they found that he had died during the night, and when they cleaned out his desk, he had not cashed the last several paychecks. Now that is commitment!

Compliance, on the other hand, means the leader gets the minimum effort. It's the "clock-watcher." It's the employee who sees challenges, but doesn't try to solve them ahead of time. It's the one who probably has great ideas, but doesn't contribute them to the team.

There is just one more thing you need to give your team for them to be committed to doing their best, and without this you won't have a team that shows what a great leader you are. It's something you can identify with, because I'll bet you want the same thing for yourself.

You need to give them meaningful work—work that challenges them and provides them the opportunity to provide and add value in whatever industry or business they pursue. Let's discuss why that is, what we often do (unwittingly) that demotivates, and how we get commitment.

Meaningful Work

For work to be meaningful to us, we need to:

- Believe we add value to the organization and get recognized and appreciated as doing so

- Be challenged—use our skills and stretch to learn new ones

- Be allowed some autonomy in our work (some people need more than others)

- Be able to see results and progress from the work we do

Value, Challenge, Autonomy and Results

In Dan Pink's book *Drive: The Surprising Truth About What Motivates Us*, he refutes the power of external motivators, and says that traditional rewards, like a year-end bonus, only gets better performance from people who do rote tasks. He says that once you start dealing with work where creative thinking is involved, there are three key motivators: (1) autonomy (self-directed work) (2) mastery (getting better at our work) and (3) purpose (serving a greater vision).[15]

In a study by Harvard University Professor Teresa Amabile, and Steven Kramer, a researcher and writer, 669 managers were surveyed around the world. They were asked to rank the importance of five employee motivators: incentives, recognition, clear goals, interpersonal support, and progress in the work. Only eight percent of the senior executives ranked progress in their work as the most important motivator. Professor Amabile says that a multiyear research project by Harvard found that "of all the events that can deeply engage people in their jobs, the single most important is making progress in meaningful work."[16]

Behavioral researcher Dan Ariely said in a recent TED talk: "We really have this incredibly simplistic view of why people work and what the labor market looks like." He goes on to cite several studies he conducted that gave evidence that we are driven by meaningful work and the acknowledgement of others that we put in a lot of effort. And he says that the harder the task, the prouder we are.

"When we think about labor, we usually think about motivation and payment as the same thing, but the reality is that we should probably add all kinds of things to it: meaning, creation, challenges, ownership, identity, pride, etc.," Ariely explains.[17]

In a study conducted at Cornell University, half of 320 small businesses they studied used old-fashioned command and control management practices, while the other half gave employees autonomy for doing their jobs. The businesses that gave autonomy grew *four times faster* than those using command and control practices, and experienced only one-third of the turnover as the ones using command and control.[18]

Or put yourself in a situation I was in. Peter didn't want to move to another division. This wasn't good news for me. We had undergone a significant reorganization, and as a result, we were precluded from hiring or promoting anyone. As Acting Division head, Peter had done a good job and was looking forward to getting the job permanently, but because of these recent events, it wasn't to be. Our higher headquarters had put a freeze on promotions. Because I was a higher grade than Peter, the Director asked me to take over as permanent Division Chief. I felt bad for him, and thought he wouldn't want to stay and work for me. He could move to another Division and I could start fresh. That, too, wasn't to be. My Director informed me that Peter wanted to stay in my division. I wasn't relishing developing a program that was in progress and that he had led.

Peter and I sat down to discuss it. I told him I knew it was a tough disappointment for him, and then I asked, "If you can't be the leader, what is the job you most want to do?" He told me that the most exciting part of the project was the technical development. It happened to be something that had not been done before, and he wanted to prove that it could be done. It just so happened that was the part of the project I liked the least!

I was glad to give Peter full reins on that development, and getting his full support on how it happened gave me the freedom to do the things I should have been doing. Peter absolutely shone in this new role, and as a result, seemed to harbor no resentment towards me. In fact, he became my biggest supporter, and I learned a valuable lesson. Had I done what I wanted to do, and insisted he move to another group, we likely would not have gotten the project done on time, nor would we have been able to show what the organization could do. Finding out what Peter's values were (freedom to create; adding value; autonomy), and ensuring he had meaningful work, made all the difference in how committed he was.

How To Know What Drives Our Team

Often as leaders (I've done this too), we pick people to work for us because they seem a lot like us. Their skills are probably different, but they seem to have our same interests. However, just because something motivates us doesn't mean it will motivate them.

Why is that? Because we aren't all the same. We all have different values—that is, those things that are important to us.

Values are simply what a person believes is important about

their life. They are the *motivation* behind what we do. Values are our priorities that tell us how to spend our time. It's who you are as a person, your Global Positioning System (GPS), what will keep you moving in the right direction when you have those days when everything seems to be going wrong (and we all have those). This is the path that guides you forward.

We choose our values freely, but they usually come from our parents, family, authority figures, and friends. They are deeply rooted—they are at our core. Out of them come our beliefs, which influence what we believe about our strengths, limitations, and other people.

Knowing our own values, and understanding our employees' values, helps us understand how to motivate them and keep their commitment. Why is that?

First of all, time is a limited resource. No matter who you are, you only get 24 hours a day. If we waste time by investing in actions and activities that don't take our lives in the direction we want, that loss is permanent. We can always earn more money, lose weight, get fitter, and try new behaviors. What we can't do is get a redo on yesterday. So planning life and time around living our values—what we believe in—is a way to ensure we are doing our best, and we get to decide what "best" means to us.

Another reason to understand our values is because we are so busy and live in such a frenetic and distracting world. We don't finish one thing before we have to work on another, and we're frequently juggling several projects at once. And that's just our work lives. Knowing what our values are helps us prioritize what gets done when it isn't possible to do it all.

And my values are different than yours. And yours are different than the people who work for you. It's not a good or bad, it's just ours—and their—"truth" about how we see the world.

"When you believe that others always see the world as you do, you'll be frustrated. You have to start from where they are. You have to speak their language," says Richard Scherberger.

When Scherberger gives leadership training, he talks about it being like ballroom dancing. In ballroom dancing, the only way you get to lead is if your partner lets you. Just like we lead our team—with commitment, not just compliance—it is because others let us. They are following instead of pulling in the other direction.

For example, let's say that Janice is one of my employees. One of Janice's values is that she is motivated by freedom. That's the value that she prizes above all others. Janice is good at her job and has been doing it a long time. How much commitment will I get from Janice if I tell her exactly what to do, and how to do it, when she has ideas of her own?

It's well worth your time to understand what drives each person, and what makes them "tick." In work, as in life, not everyone stays on top of their game all the time. We will all have days like this. Changes in the workplace will, sooner or later, give you some challenges. You may wonder if your team is off course. When these times happen, and they will, commitment from your team members will get you through.

You and your team can take a values survey to find out what

drives each person, and it makes for a great team-building discussion and activity. I've included information on some options in the Resources Section.

When We De-Motivate

We all need a positive work life, both inside ourselves (how we feel about our work) as well as work that we believe is meaningful. Some days we feel we are making headway, getting support, overcoming obstacles, and having great ideas that drive us to succeed. But on those days when we feel we are spinning our wheels and encountering roadblocks, our motivation is lowest. It is no different for our employees.

Maybe you have had times when something happened that, even temporarily, completely de-motivated you. I know I have.

I wasn't chosen.

NASA had a new Administrator, the top spot, and after a three-year period of upheaval following the Columbia accident, we were anxious that once again we were going to go through changes. We were all curious about him, what his philosophy was, and how it would affect us.

As the last of 10 centers to get a personal visit, we had plenty of information from the other centers on how their visits went. As one of the C-suite executives, it was probably going to be my only opportunity to meet him, and the others on the executive team felt the same. As time approached, we cleared our calendars so we would be available. The day before the visit, we were all told by our leader that, typically for us I'm sorry

CHAPTER 7

to say, "We will do it differently than everyone else." Only two or three selected (and the implication was those most important) executives would get to meet with him. And the "why" was never explained. Although some of the other execs complained, I had been around long enough to realize this would do no good, but it did serve to alert me that job satisfaction probably wasn't going to happen for this phase of my career! Although I chalked it up to having an inexperienced leader who didn't understand how it affected us all, it was a great lesson for me: *Try never to de-motivate my employees by not explaining things that may be important to them, and never forget to remind them they are important to my organization.*

In the book, *The Progress Principle*, Amabile and Kramer say, "Managers at all levels routinely—and unwittingly—undermine the meaningfulness of work for their direct subordinates through everyday words and actions." They cite things we often do, such as failing to acknowledge or dismissing the importance of subordinates' work or ideas; destroying our employees' sense of ownership in work by switching people off project teams before their work is completed; changing goals so frequently that employees feel they will never be finished, and neglecting to keep them up to date on changing priorities.[18]

They also say that even though a higher level leader may have fewer opportunities to directly affect their employees' inner work lives than first-line managers, the smallest actions can pack a wallop because what you say and do as a leader is intensely observed by people down the line.

A top leader is always on display and always being observed— and a sense of purpose about the work has to come from the top.

When it comes to recommendations for leaders, Amabile and Kramer don't mince words: "Scrupulously avoid impeding progress by changing goals autocratically, being indecisive, or holding up resources. In short, this means we should give our team members what they need to thrive, and then get out of the way."[19]

Sometimes we are so busy looking at strategy, delivering on plans, and solving problems we can forget to do that. The secret is paying attention, and recognizing when people are doing a good job.

One manager I read about said that with all the demands of her work days, which included back-to-back meetings, it was sometimes impossible to recognize achievements. She often found herself working after hours alone, just to catch up. She told the story that one night after a particularly hard week, she wrote personalized thank-you notes on sticky pads and stuck them on everyone's computer screens. She was surprised at the reaction the next morning. People were coming into her office to thank her because it meant so much to them.

We all want to feel valued. Research has proven time and time again that the most powerful motivators for people are their achievements and the recognition of them. And when those achievements are recognized by their leaders, they do amazing things. As Vince Lombardi said, "Individual commitment to a group effort — that is what makes a team work, a company work, a society work, a civilization work."

How Am I Doing On Getting Commitment?

1. What am I doing to make my employees feel valued?

2. Does everyone on my team have meaningful work that they are fully engaged in?

3. Do my managers provide employees with appropriate autonomy or are they micromanaging?

4. Do I know what my employees hold as their values?

5. Do I have any de-motivators, either work or supervisors?

CHAPTER 8
Lagniappe

It's never crowded along the extra mile.
– Dr. Wayne Dyer

You made it through the book! You know the five steps to building a great team or organization. I hope you have tried some of them already.

I call this chapter "lagniappe" because it's a little something extra. This is a bonus chapter in the print book that I have not yet included in the digital version. I wanted to give you some extra help on issues I hear my clients say trouble them-- practical tools you can use right away to be a better leader and to get the most out of your team.

First we will discuss how to brainstorm with your team. In Chapter 4 I mentioned brainstorming. This is a great way to get ideas from your team; however, how to do it is often mis-understood. There are some key parameters that will help you get better ideas than you have generated before.

Second, we will talk about how you can make the dreaded performance yearly counseling session one that will be pro-ductive, positive, and helpful.

Then I will give you some additional helpful insights on ensuring you are making good decisions.

What is Brainstorming and Why Use It?

An analytical problem-solving model is important to every organization; however, we often get stuck with our "same ole, same old" solutions. Every now and then it's important to approach a new challenge by getting new and imaginative ideas. Brainstorming is one technique that can bring a richness of ideas and get us buy-in from team members for the solution chosen – after all, they're likely to be more committed to an approach if they were involved in developing it.

What's more, because brainstorming is fun, when done right it helps team members bond as they solve problems in a positive, rewarding environment. If we do it without judgment, we get fresh ideas no one has thought of. Being asked to brainstorm ideas also helps you get buy-in for new ideas because they helped create them, and makes your team feel valuable when they are listened to without judgment. Brainstorming exercises are great team building exercises when they are done in a casual, relaxed and non-judgmental setting.

How to Brainstorm For Great Ideas

When we think we are brainstorming, we often believe that means we just sit at a table or in a room with others and toss out ideas. Although that's true, it's far from complete. The most important thing for creating new ideas is people's imagination. We want to jolt their creativity by putting people in a relaxed atmosphere and encouraging them to come up with lots of idea—the more and zanier the better. Too often we "analyze" the ideas while we are brainstorming and end up squelching some of the best ones because we judge too quickly and make people feel they cannot speak up for fear of looking stupid. We have all attended "brainstorming" sessions where some potentially brilliant nuggets of great ideas never come to light because they are dismissed outright, or discouraged because they aren't explored.

How We Can Brainstorm Better

In the process of brainstorming for great ideas, the most important thing is to get them out of people's heads and recorded. We will analyze which ones to explore later. It's important to remember:

- Define the problem. Before you begin to brainstorm for ideas, ensure you have captured the real problem you want to solve.

- Prepare the group. Besides giving the group the problem you will solve ahead of time (so they will come in with ideas), ensure you have a variety of people as attendees. It's difficult to generate new and different ideas if everyone at the session tends to think alike. Prepare the room to be open and have a relaxed atmosphere.

- Guide the discussion. It's recommended to have a facilitator to keep things fun and moving in the right direction. The facilitator can set the stage, and encourage the group to not only give out their own ideas, but develop other people's ideas, and use them to create new ideas.

Building on others' ideas is one of the most valuable aspects of group brainstorming.

- No idea is a bad idea. Set up the rule at the beginning of the brainstorming session that there will be no "killer phrases" (see those below). It's easy for us as humans to quickly dismiss ideas we believe are unworthy of attention, but often just listening to them helps us think of other, related ideas that may turn out to be the best ones.

- The crazier and wilder an idea sounds, the better. The idea itself might not work (or it might if we don't judge too quickly), but it could lead to another idea that no one has thought of.

- Strive for quantity at the first pass around the room, not quality. Get as many ideas as you can out on the table and in writing.

- Write down every idea, either posted with sticky notes on a board at the front of the room or by a recorder who has been designated to take notes. If you use sticky notes, have someone transcribe all the ideas so everyone has a copy and can see them. Sticky notes are a good idea because people can write down ideas and not have them attributed to them out loud. Sometimes this helps the introverts participate better.

- Draw out the ideas of introverts. There are several ways to do this. You can call on them throughout the session (but not first—give them time to think), or ask everyone to be ready with ideas the day before. Introverts need time to process and "warm up" before they are willing to share. The sticky-note idea above often helps them do that.

- Do the analysis separately from the brainstorming. There is something really creative about putting aside the ideas and analyzing at a different time. When it's time to analyze the ideas, I encourage you to set the parameters for analysis, rank-ordered by what is most important. For example, some of the rankings may be cost to implement, time to implement, level of approval to implement, ease to implement, or effect on other systems. You can even rank-order in different categories and then look at the alternatives with fresh eyes.

Killer Phrases

There are some phrases to be careful of. Let everyone know up front that these aren't allowed for the initial brainstorming session:

- "That might be a good idea, but…."
- "That's not our job."
- "You've got to be kidding!"
- "The boss will never buy it."
- "That's against company policy."
- "That's not practical."
- "That will cost too much."
- "We tried that before."
- "It will never work."
- "That's a stupid idea."

Performance Counseling Without Pain

In Step 1, Making the Connection, you learned that performance counseling, that yearly or twice-yearly meeting where employees are given a "rating" according to a company policy or regulation, is not the way to make a connection with your people. A more frequent meeting where you get to know your employee is much more effective, and will help the more formal performance counseling session go much smoother.

What Is Performance Counseling?

In many larger organizations or agencies, it is a requirement that each employee must have (at least) an annual performance counseling session. It does not need to be something a leader dreads doing. When used in conjunction with the meetings you have already had, it can be smooth and easy, and can help you get even more information to help you and the employee plan their career.

This type performance meeting is mostly for the well-performing employee. When there is a real and consistent performance problem, this is not the meeting for that—there should have already been a series of meetings and discussions. This meeting should never be the first time your employee has heard there is a performance problem (see Chapter 6, "When Things Must Improve.")

The problem with performance counseling sessions is that leaders often feel performance counseling is a pro forma meeting. It's something they have to do, and their biggest issue is just getting through it. They aren't comfortable with conducting this kind of meeting. Most of us don't use it to connect with employees or use it to actually help that employee improve performance.

We can, however, use it to guide our employees in their career paths, and gain information that will help us plan for this employee's work for the entire year. It can also help us realize who needs training, what kind, when, and if they are ready for additional assignments.

How We Can Do Performance Counseling Better

Just as for other meetings, it's important to set some time aside so you aren't just asking them to sign their appraisal. Your employees deserve feedback, and they are looking to you as their leader to provide how they can navigate their career through the company.

It's also important to plan which questions are appropriate ahead of time so that it doesn't become too structured and formal. A relaxed and informal atmosphere will help them open up and help you gain better information.

Here are some suggested questions to ask during performance counseling:

- What aspects of your job do you like best? What aspects of your job do you like least?

- If you were the leader, what are some ideas you have for improving this organization?

- In your judgment, who are the most innovative, committed, and helpful of your teammates?

- Who are the most innovative, committed, and helpful of people outside our direct team?

- What do you believe are your chances for promotion to the next level, and during what time frame?

- What do you believe you need to do (training, projects, etc.) to get you ready for promotion?

- What job would you aspire to next and why?

- What personal goals have you set for yourself?

- What self-improvement goals or projects have you undertaken to get yourself ready for promotion?

- Where do you see yourself in five years?

- What are the top three things that we do here that seems to be a waste of time, redundant, or of little value to the organization?

- On a scale of 1 to 10, with 10 being best, what number would you give to rank this organization? Why?

- If you could work on a different project or have a developmental assignment in a different office to broaden your skills and improve your career, what would it be?

- Do you feel well trained for your duties? Where do you feel you need additional training?

- What do I, as the leader, do that wastes your time?

- What bothers you most about my leadership style and decisions?

As the leader, you are going to want to be ready to listen to feedback from your employees, and sincerely want to hear it, especially with those last two questions. Otherwise, don't ask them. These questions are a good way, however, to find out how your style appeals to your team, how your decisions are viewed (they often didn't understand why you made them), and how you can be more effective as a leader.

Please don't forget to thank them for answering all the questions, and let them know you will use this information to help them better guide their careers.

Making Good Decisions

Being a leader means we have to make lots of decisions. When you teach your employees to take responsibility and make decisions that you have entrusted to them, it saves the really key or sensitive decisions for you to spend your time on. I have found that generally, many leaders try to do too much by themselves and find it hard to delegate. If leaders try to do too much by themselves, they will accomplish less and feel more stress.

How We Can Improve Our Decision Making

Most often, we won't know immediately if we have made a good decision. In these cases, we need to develop a confidence in ourselves that we have considered all the options and made the best decision we can with the information we have. I have seen experienced (and not so experienced) leaders almost frozen in their ability to make decisions, because they feel they don't have perfect data. One thing to remember: You will seldom, if ever, have all the data you need to be sure your decision is the correct one.

Here is a good guide for you to use to improve your confidence when you must make an important decision:

- Is it time to make this decision? I like to ask: "Has it cooked enough?" That is, you may not have all the facts, but do you have enough of them to ensure that the right people have been coordinated with, and the relevant data available has been researched, by you or by one of your staff members?

- Does it make sense? I loved the analogy I read one time in a great book, *Rules & Tools for Leaders*, by MG Perry M. Smith (Retired). When talking about a decision making challenge, he said, "Have we created a thoroughbred race horse, a plodding but sturdy farm horse, or a camel with ten humps? The farm horse may be the best you can get, and you may have to be satisfied with that, but don't accept the camel." If we need to reject it and give additional guidance, then we should take the time to do that.

- Is it ethical? Will the decision I'm making enhance our reputation as an organization? Is it a decision we can be proud of in terms of integrity while still moving forward our goals?

- What else/who else will it effect? Does it make sense in terms of its effect on other systems and the rest of the organization?

- The *Washington Post* check. This is a term we used to

apply in the Pentagon: How would this decision look like if it were reported in the *Washington Post* headlines? It often helped remind us as leaders that anything we decide is going to be scrutinized by outsiders who didn't understand the background.

- Will it help or hurt? Does this decision affect the safety, health or well-being of employees, stakeholders or customers? Will it help or hurt morale?

- Is this decision consistent with other decisions I've made? If not, what do I need to do to explain my change in direction so my employees are behind me?

- Will this decision help or hurt the future of the organization? When we look at the big picture, will my decision help the short-term issue but hurt us long-term? Will we need to change the strategic plan, goals, or priorities of the organization? This may be the right thing to do, but it must be considered.

- How and in what way will I communicate the decision?

Every decision won't apply to all these questions, but if you get used to asking them when you make decisions, I believe you will make better decisions and be able to explain the ones you make in a way that will convince your leaders and followers that yours are well thought out.

CHAPTER 9
Your Leadership Challenge

Meet your people where they are. They may not be as good as they can be, but they are as good as they believe they can be.
– Susan Chandler Foster

A s a leader or aspiring leader, you now have the skills you need to build a committed, creative and inspired team or organization.

You know that the people who work for you—your biggest resource—need and want you to be the leader who:

- Makes a personal connection and lets them know you care about them

- Is trustworthy

- Will say what you mean and mean what you say

- Will listen deeply

- Appreciates them and lets them know

You know that they also want meaningful work, and they want to do a good job. Just like you, every person who works for you is only as great as *they believe* they can be.

They need you to lead them and show them the possibilities

for your organization and for their accomplishments.

You may have heard these skills called the "soft skills," but you will find that they aren't always easy to master when you have stresses and are busy. They are like any other skills, however. You can learn them, practice them, and own them.

You can do this. ***This isn't rocket science!***

You can be the best strategist in the world, and not be a great leader. I firmly believe there is no method for great leadership outside of building the right relationship with your team that will enable you to build a great organization.

You may have been taught somewhere along the way, either by a boss or some college curriculum, that *getting the job done, no matter what it takes* is the way to get ahead as a leader. This could very well work in the short run, but I can tell you for a fact, as a recovering 24 hour-a-day, 7 day-a-week "workaholic," that it isn't sustainable—either for you or your team.

You will have days with challenges. You and your team may go through reorganizations, times of financial stress, or other kinds of upheavals. You may have to deal with difficult customers or an occasional employee who just doesn't fit, no matter what you try.

I want you to know you can go through these times confidently, because you have learned the leadership skills that will make you more valuable than the average person who goes through them.

Mastering the Skills

Mentally preparing yourself, as part of learning a skill, is well documented in many professions. The Navy Seals, astronauts, and professional sports teams all do it. But they also train and practice. Just thinking isn't enough—you have to also do it. To build your confidence, I invite you to practice. I also invite you to:

See yourself as a leader. Being a supervisor or manager does not make you a leader. You get to decide to be a leader. It was Peter Drucker who said, "Management is doing things right; leadership is doing the right things." And if you are not a formal leader yet, look for opportunities to practice these skills, and when you get the chance, you will be ready.

John Quincy Adams said, "If your actions inspire others to dream more, learn more, do more and become more, you are a leader."

You are a leader if you say you are. Claim that.

When you seem stuck, ask yourself, "What is the story I am telling myself in this situation?"

My client, David, was one of the executives in a team I coached. When I met with him for the first time, he told me his biggest problem was he had a difficult team. David was stressed because he was too busy, and had too much work, and they weren't helping him enough. When we began to break down the team's problems, I asked him if he was meeting with them one-on-one to discuss them, and delegate work to them. David insisted he didn't have time because the company was reorganizing. Since I was coaching the other execs too, I knew they were reorganizing, yet none of the other team had used that problem as an excuse.

With my encouragement, he made a plan for some ways he could work that into his schedule, and he vowed to try them. A few weeks later when it was time for a follow-up, he and I met again. We could have recorded David's first session and played it again. His team was difficult and he was too busy. When I asked him how the one-on-one regular meetings had helped, David said he hadn't been able to implement any of our ideas because the company had a budget shortfall. Are you seeing a pattern here?

After coaching this team a few more weeks, David gave me yet another excuse as to why he hadn't tried anything on his plan, and I confronted him. These may have been his actual circumstances, but they weren't the reason he wasn't meeting with his team or delegating work.

David was telling himself the same story, so he stayed stuck. And when the story no longer worked, he changed it. I challenged him to reframe that story, decide whether or not he was serious about connecting with them, delegate the work that belonged to them, and either fix the issues or quit complaining about them. David realized he had let his story about his people and about his time affect how he was leading.

How do we know if it's a story? If it's a fact, there is concrete evidence that can be proven by anyone observing the situation. For example, if I tell you I don't have enough money, that's a story. You have no idea how much I have or how much I need. If I tell you I have five dollars in my purse, you can observe that. Whether it's enough money depends on what you need to buy and what part of the world you live in. When we reframe the story, we can find better solutions.

Don't expect perfection. You won't necessarily have a "win" every day. Some things you do and the seeds you sow, you may not see the results of while you are in that job. When you blow it, admit it and move on. Don't aim for perfection—aim for progress. I had a leader tell me one time he'd fire anyone who told him they had failed. Then I asked him to please give me his story on a period of time where he had been perfect. I never did get that story. Remember, these are skills and behaviors, and you can learn them, practice them, and develop them.

Get help when you need it. Practice with a friend or family member. Write down what you need to say before a meeting. Mentally rehearse those important meetings ahead of time. Get a coach if you need to, or one for your team. There are thousands of coaches out there. I encourage you to find one who will help you build up your team, and not just work on the typical things like goal setting and improving your business processes.

Get support from your leaders. Share with them what you are doing to improve your team and ask for support. You may just start a movement.

The Challenge

Your job as the leader is to get people to follow you from where they are to where they need to be. There is, in my opinion, no greater calling, whether you are leading a country, an organization, a community, a family, or yourself.

As an organizational, team or business leader, keeping people motivated to be their best is the most important thing you will do, aside from developing them. It's your job to see greatness in them, even when they can't see it in themselves.

I invite you to try on these new skills for 30 days with your team. I firmly believe that at the end of these 30 days, you will see a tremendous and measurable difference in your team.

I want to hear how you are doing. I want to hear about your challenges, your stories (both what worked and didn't). I'm only an email away at susan@susancfoster.com.

Kevin Eikenberry, author of *Remarkable Leadership*, said: "Deep down you know you can be remarkable. You shouldn't settle for anything less than your best self, reaching ever closer to your potential — whether as a leader or in any other part of your life."

Yours in leadership,

Susan

NOTES

1. State of the American Workplace: Employee Engagement Insights for U. S. Business Leaders, Gallup, Inc., 2013. http://employeeengagement.com/wp-content/uploads/2013/06/Gallup-2013-State-of-the-American-Workplace-Report.pdf

2. Forbes.com, "Make More Money By Making Your Employees Happy," by Steve Cooper, 7/30/2012

3. "A CCL Research White Paper: The Stress of Leadership," by Michael Campbell, Jessica Innis Baites, Andre Martin, and Kyle Meddings, Center for Creative Leadership, 2007.

4. Harvard Business Review: "Connect, Then Lead," by Amy J. C. Cuddy, Matthew Kohut, and John Neffinger, July 2013

5. Emotional Intelligence: Peter Salovey, Yale University, and John D. Mayer, University of New Hampshire, 1990, Baywood Publishing Company, Inc.

6. Consortium for Research on Emotional Intelligence in Organizations, www.eiconsortium.org. Reprinted with permission.

7. Covey, Stephen M. R., *The Speed of Trust: The One Thing That Changes Everything*, Free Press, February 2008.

8. Chicagotribune.com, "Rebuilding Trust at Work: From snippiness to lying, office betrayals can break professional relationships," by Jen Weigel, April 11, 2011

9. Michael Hyatt, http://michaelhyatt.com/why-vision-is-more-important-than-strategy.html

10. Harvard Business Review, Sept 2004 issue, "Stop Wasting Valuable Time," by Michael C. Mankins.

11. Columbia Accident Investigation Board report, August 2003, www.nasa.gov/columbia/home/CAIB_Vol1.html

12. Gallup Business Journal, November 9, 2006, "In Praise of Praising Your Employees," by Jennifer Robinson.

13. Harvard Business Review, January 2014, by Jack Zenger and Joseph Folkman, https://hbr.org/2014/01/your-employees-want-the-negative-feedback-you-hate-to-give/

14. Gallup Study: Impact of Manager Feedback, by Leslie Allan, Feb 22, 2011 http://hr.toolbox.com/blogs/people-at-work/gallup-study-impact-of-manager-feedback-on-employee-engagement-43509

15. Pink, Daniel H. Drive: *The Surprising Truth Behind What Motivates Us*, Riverhead Books, April 2011

16. McKinsey & Company, McKinsey Quarterly: "Insights & Publications," *How leaders kill meaning at work*, January 2012, by Teresa Amabile and Steven Kramer

17. Ariely, Dan: http://blog.ted.com/2013/04/10/what-motivates-us-at-work-7-fascinating-studies-that-give-insights/

18. Amabile, Teresa and Steven Kramer, "The Progress Principle: Using Small Wins to Ignite Joy, Engagement, and

Creativity at Work," Harvard Business Review Press, July 19, 2011.

19. Amabile, Teresa and Steven Kramer, "The power of small wins," *Harvard Business Review*, May 2011, Volume 89, Number 5.

RESOURCES

Organization and Leadership Development

Executive Leadership Skills, International
112 Martingale Circle
Madison, Alabama 35758
www.els1.com
Richard Scherberger
1-800-793-4809

<u>Emotional Intelligence</u>
Consortium for Research on Emotional Intelligence in Organizations, www.eiconsortium.org.

Books

Getting to Yes, Roger Fisher and William Ury, Penguin Books, 2011

7 Habits of Highly Effective People, Stephen Covey, Rosetta-Books, 2013 (25th Anniversary Edition)

The Virgin Way: Everything I Know About Leadership, by Richard Branson, Portfolio (September 9, 2014)

The Speed of Trust: The One Thing That Changes Everything, Stephen M. R. Covey, Free Press; Reprint edition (February 5, 2008)

The Trust Edge: How Top Leaders Gain Faster Results, Deeper Relationships, and a Stronger Bottom Line, David Horsager, Free Press, Oct 9, 2012

Conversational Intelligence: How Great Leaders Build Trust & Get Extraordinary Results, Bibliomotion, Oct 1, 2013

Rebuilding Trust in the Workplace: Seven Steps to Renew Confidence, Commitment, and Energy, Dennis Reina and Michella Reina, Berrett-Koeler Publishers (September 7, 2010)

1501 Ways to Reward Employees, now in a new edition entitled *1501 Ways to Reward Employees*, Dr. Bob Nelson, Workman Publishing Company; Reprint edition (March 27, 2012)

Drive: The Surprising Truth About What Motivates Us, Daniel H. Pink, Riverhead Books (April 5, 2011)

Values Surveys

For Teams:

Recalibrate Values Cards

"Recalibrate Cards are an extremely powerful and fun way for leaders to increase their levels of personal leadership effectiveness because they show leaders how to quickly and effectively determine the best ways to lead their teams. They help build trust, they open up communication channels, and they create lifelong impact on the people that use them. Any trainer or facilitator can use these to help dramatically increase excitement, engagement, and most importantly, retention with their existing training content."

http://www.recalibratecards.com/Recalibrate-Cards.php

For Teams and Individuals:

Rokeach Values Survey. (See Executive Leadership Skills, International (above))

About the Author

Susan Chandler Foster is a Master Certified Coach and unshakeable optimist who believes everyone can learn to be a great leader. A recovering 24/7 workaholic who helps overwhelmed leaders get the best from their organizations and teams, she honed her leadership skills as a leader for over 25 years with NASA and the U. S. Army. Her advice has been quoted in such publications as *Business Insider Daily* and *Career-Intelligence.net*. She holds a Masters Degree from the University of Southern California and is a graduate of the U. S. Army War College.

Her website is: www.susancfoster.com

Thank You

Thank you for reading this book. Two things I believe: (1) I believe you can be a great leader, and (2) I believe we can heal our organizations from the huge amount of the stress and build better ones by building great leaders.

What's next:

- I encourage you to take the Leadership Challenge for 30 days. I'd love to hear how it goes for you, any questions or concerns as you undertake it, and what your results are.
- There wasn't space in this book for me to include everything I wanted to talk about in being a great leader. Please go to my website and look under the Tab marked "Book" for downloadable worksheets:
    - o How Well Do I Know My Employees—I invite you to fill out one on each of your direct reports and keep it where you can have it handy for one-on-one meetings with them
    - o Reflection Questions at the end of each chapter
    - o Coaching Worksheet to help you craft those difficult conversations when we need specific behaviors to change.
- Sign up on my website to get my blog on a regular basis, as we talk about being a great leader and building great organizations.

Susan C. Foster
Contact Information

Website
www.susancfoster.com

LinkedIn
https://www.linkedin.com/Susan (Chandler) Foster

Facebook
https://www.facebook.com/susanfostercoaching

Twitter
https://www.twitter.com/LeaderCoach1

Email
susan@susancfoster.com